THE SUN AND THE MOON

Text by Dr. Gary Mechler, with Melinda Hutson and Dr. Robert Marcialis
Alfred A. Knopf, New York

Contents

How to Use This Guide

The Sun and the Moon are the celestial objects with which we are most familiar. This guide will help turn your acquaintance with these bodies into knowledge. You will learn why eclipses, auroras, and other celestial events happen as well as how to observe the Sun safely and how to identify geographical features on the Moon.

Organization

This easy-to-use pocket guide is divided into three parts: introductory essays, illustrated accounts on features of the Sun and the Moon, and appendices.

Introduction

The introductory essay "The Solar System" explains how the Sun and the nine planets came into being billions of years ago. "The Sun, Our Star" explains what type of star our Sun is and how it produces energy, and describes its atmosphere and its magnetic activity. "The Double Planet" is an essay about Earth and its Moon, discussing how the Moon formed, its motions in the sky, its phases, and its tidal pull on Earth. "Observing the Sun" explains how to observe the Sun safely, and "Observing the Moon" discusses the best times and ways to study the Moon.

The Sun and the Moon

This section includes 79 color and black-and-white illustrations, images, and photographs of the Sun and solar phenomena and of the Moon, each accompanied by a detailed text description. The Sun section covers the Sun as it appears in the sky, the Sun in the solar system, the Sun as a star, the structure and individual features of the Sun, eclipses, and optical effects caused by sunlight or solar radiation. The Moon section covers the phases of the Moon, lunar eclipses, and the Moon's topography on both the nearside and the farside. Lunar maps accompany photographs of the Moon at first- and third-quarter phases, providing detailed illustrations of the nearside surface. For quick reference, a black-and-white drawing identifies the subject or phenomenon covered. These are explained in the Key to the Color Plates.

Appendices   "Solar Imaging" explains some of the methods used to obtain images of the Sun. Tables provide basic data on the Sun and the Moon and list the solar and lunar eclipses that will occur from 1995 to 2010. An index follows the tables.

The Solar System

The observable, physical universe is comprised of billions of galaxies. Our Sun is one of countless billions of stars in the Milky Way galaxy, a flat disk of stars 100,000 light-years across. Our solar system is in the disk about 27,000 light-years from the center. We are orbiting the galactic center at a rate of 250 km (155 miles) per second, completing one orbit every 220 million years.

The Sun is at the center of our solar system. Revolving around the Sun are the nine planets—Mercury, Venus, Earth, Mars, Jupiter, Saturn, Uranus, Neptune, and Pluto (to remember their order, memorize the line "*M*y *V*ery *E*ducated *M*other *J*ust *S*erved *U*s *N*ine *P*ickles"); their satellites, including our Moon; a large number of minor planets (asteroids), most of which occur in the asteroid belt, an orbital band between the orbits of Mars and Jupiter; and innumerable meteoroids and comets.

Formation

Scientists have developed theories about the formation of our solar system by observing its present-day structure and motions, which are artifacts of its origin. New stars forming in our galaxy provide firsthand evidence of a process that is essentially identical to the one that formed our own star and its attendant planets.

About 4.6 billion years ago, a large tenuous nebula—an interstellar cloud of gases (mostly hydrogen and helium) and dust (carbon, silicon, and iron)—reacted to the inward pull of its own weight and slowly began to collapse. At some point, the collapse was hastened by the impact of a shock wave of material blasted by a nearby exploding star. The new materials swirled and mixed—incompletely—with the collapsing cloud. As material fell to the center, the spin rate of the cloud increased, flattening it into a disk. This cloud, now thick with dust, formed one giant whirlpool, with some material falling farther inward and faster into orbit than other material. Small whirlpools and eddies collected materials that began to stick together, building up globules so massive that gravity within them began to squeeze the material inward, warming it. Thus, around 4.55 billion years ago, the planets of the solar system were coming into being. The central mass, the proto-sun, of the 6-billion-mile-diameter disk was beginning to compress itself so greatly with the infall of huge quantities of matter that its heat began to radiate with an orange-red glow. The heat baked the inner planets into small, hard, dense spheres. Those in outer, cooler regions retained their gases and became the gas giants we know today.

The Sun, Our Star

The Sun is our local star. It is of average mass, size, composition, and brightness, but its nearness (only about 150 million km/93 million miles from Earth) makes it appear large and bright. Its light reaches us in a little more than eight minutes. The next nearest star, Proxima Centauri, is about 270,000 times farther away, and its light takes more than four years to reach us.

Spectral Types

Astronomers have devised a system of classification that groups stars by *spectral type,* based on the strengths and positions of absorption lines in their spectra. These lines, as with stellar colors, are a function of temperature and, to a lesser extent, atmospheric pressure. Astronomers deduce size (from the pressure effect) and surface (atmospheric) temperature by studying a star's spectrum, and then calculate the energy output (luminosity), which depends upon temperature and surface area. Since the absorption lines are formed by atoms, astronomers can deduce stars' chemical compositions as well.

From hottest to coolest (bluest to reddest) the seven major spectral types are O, B, A, F, G, K, M (a mnemonic device for remembering these is "*O*h, *B*e *A F*ine *G*irl/*G*uy, *K*iss *M*e").

Each major spectral type is divided into a number of subtypes, from 0 to 9 (hotter to cooler). The hottest, bluest stars are of spectral type O4 or O5; the coolest, reddest stars are of type M8 or M9. The Sun's G2 classification tells us it is a yellowish-white star with a surface temperature of about 5,800° Kelvin. To classify a star as, say, a tiny white dwarf or a supergiant, astronomers have assigned each type a *luminosity class*, denoted by Roman numerals (and sometimes lowercase letters), which can range from Ia (bright supergiant) to VII (white dwarf). The full spectral type of a star consists of its temperature class plus its luminosity class. The Sun's luminosity class, V, tells us it is a normal, main sequence star.

The Sun's Energy

For most of its lifetime a star gets its energy from nuclear fusion, by converting four hydrogen nuclei (protons) into a single helium nucleus. The mass of the helium nucleus is 0.7 percent less than the sum of the masses of the four hydrogen nuclei. That tiny fraction of mass is converted into large amounts of energy ($E = mc^2$) by the nuclear reactions occurring in the star's core. Stars in this phase of life, when they burn hydrogen fuel, are called *main sequence stars*. Our Sun has been in this phase for about

4.5 billion years and has another 5 billion years to go before it exhausts its hydrogen supply and must resort to burning heavier elements. Each second, the Sun converts a stupefying 5 million tons of hydrogen atoms into energy, an amount equivalent to the explosion of 100 billion one-megaton nuclear bombs. The Sun's energy production occurs at its core, where the extremely high temperatures (about 15 million°K) and pressure (250 billion times that of Earth's atmosphere) allow such nuclear reactions.

Most of the mass of the Sun is a huge gaseous blanket around the core. The density of the core is more than eight times that of gold, but the material there is still gaseous because of the intensely hot temperatures (in fact, it is plasma, or ionized gas). Energy from the core heats the Sun's surface, which is not solid, although it appears opaque.

The Sun's Atmosphere   The apparent surface of the Sun is the *photosphere* layer of its atmosphere. Just above it lies the *chromosphere* and above that, the *corona*, both of which are visible only with special telescopes or during eclipses of the Sun. The corona is divided into inner and outer coronas. The Sun's surface is a patchwork of turbulent cells of gas, called *granules*, that transfer heat from the interior. *Prominences,* huge loops of gases, may rise from the surface and extend far into space, then pour back along bright, arc-like magnetic fields. Also present are relatively small spikes of gas called *spicules* and occasional bright patches called *plages*. Sometimes *solar flares,* violent eruptions of matter and energy, blast light, ions, and electrons into space.

The Solar Magnetic Activity Cycle

Concentrations of magnetic fields running through the photospheric plasma cause darkened splotches on the photosphere known as *sunspots,* which are up to 1,500°K cooler than surrounding regions and thus appear black in comparison. Sunspot activity is the most readily visible manifestation of the solar magnetic activity cycle (MAC). This cycle results in peaks in the numbers of sunspots and flares every 11 years, on average.

The charged atomic particles blasted out by the Sun often reach Earth's atmosphere (especially in peak years), causing various effects: auroras, disruption and static in radio and television communications, and short circuits in electrical power grids. The solar MAC appears to affect the strength of Earth's ozone layer as well as climate, but no exact correlation has yet been confirmed.

The Double Planet

The Moon is so sizable in relation to its parent planet that together Earth and Moon make a double planet system. Only Pluto and its single satellite, Charon, are closer to each other in size. The rest of the planets that have moons dwarf their satellites as the Sun dwarfs the planets. The unusually high mass and size ratios (satellite to planet) for the Earth-Moon and Pluto-Charon systems imply that there were exceptional circumstances involved in their formation.

Origin of the Moon

The *collision ejecta theory* is the latest attempt by astronomers to explain our Moon's origin. About 4.55 billion years ago, the forming solar system was a turbulent and violent place, with ever-larger objects careening about, nudging one another with their gravities, and sometimes colliding. The theory proposes that a planetesimal (almost-planet), about half the diameter of Earth and one-tenth its mass, struck Earth at an oblique angle, blasting material from the outer rocky mantle and sending the shattered planetesimal into orbit around Earth. In a relatively short period of time this orbiting debris clumped together to form the Moon, which most likely was molten at first, then cooled and solidifed. It was battered by meteoroids and underwent a period of lava flows on the surface, which ended about 3.1 billion years ago. Since then our barren companion has remained essentially unchanged.

Motion of the Moon

All objects gravitationally bound to one another orbit around a common center of gravity (c.o.g.), a "balance point," whose specific distance from the objects is determined by the ratio of their masses. The mass ratio of the Earth-Moon system is 81:1, so the c.o.g.'s distance from Earth's center is $\frac{1}{81}$ of the distance from Earth to the Moon. The average distance of 384,400 km (239,000 miles) divided by 81 equals about 4,750 km (2,950 miles). The radius of Earth is about 6,400 km (4,000 miles), placing the c.o.g. of Earth and the Moon inside Earth. Although technically the two bodies circle a third point, for practical purposes it can be said that the Moon orbits Earth.

The Moon's orbit is complex, not a simple ellipse, because the Sun, the other planets, and Earth all pull on it. The Moon rotates on its axis in the same amount of time it takes to circle Earth, so one side of the Moon always faces us. This situation is referred to as *tidal*

15

lock or *synchronous rotation.* Actually more than half—about 59 percent—of the Moon's surface is revealed to us because of a slight oscillation of the Moon known as *libration.* The 41 percent on the opposite side, or farside, is never seen from Earth. The farside is not the "dark side," however, since the Moon does rotate, exposing all parts of its surface to sunlight over a one-month period.

Phases of the Moon

It helps in understanding the relationship between the phases of the Moon and its position relative to the Sun to remember that moonlight is reflected sunlight. At *new moon,* the Moon is positioned approximately between the Sun and Earth (but not exactly, except during solar eclipses, because of the two bodies' slightly different orbital planes). Thus, at new moon the illuminated side is facing away from Earth and the Moon is invisible to us; we are looking at its night side in our day sky, since it is very close to the direction of the Sun. Each day the Moon moves about 13° eastward in the sky in its monthly orbit.

After new moon a thin crescent appears in the southwestern sky at evening twilight as the Moon's orbital motion takes it eastward, and we see the edge of its day side. As the Moon continues in its orbit the crescent shape grows to a half moon at *first quarter* and on through *gibbous* ("humpbacked") to *full moon*. The Moon is said to be *waxing* (growing) during this half of its orbit. The Moon then *wanes* through its orbit's second half as it becomes smaller and returns to new moon phase. The entire cycle takes a *synodic month* (29.53 days). The waxing Moon is in our evening sky; the waning Moon is in our morning sky.

Tidal Effect Two large bodies, such as Earth and the Moon, exert gravitational pulls on each other. The side of Earth that is nearer to the Moon experiences a stronger pull from the Moon than Earth's farside does. This unequal force stretches Earth in the Moon's direction. (For simplicity, the Sun's role is ignored here.) Earth, being solid, doesn't stretch much (less than a foot), but the oceans do lift up toward the Moon (about two feet). Earth's rotation brings this resulting bulge past any given coastline twice in about a day's time, causing the tides.

Observing the Sun

The Sun appears to us as a blinding white disk when it is high in a clear sky. *Never attempt to look directly at the unfiltered Sun; severe and permanent eye damage can result.* You can sometimes view the Sun through a filter of atmospheric dust and gases or clouds. Seen through thick clouds or filtered through the atmosphere at sunrise or sunset, the Sun's disk usually appears featureless. Rarely, very large sunspots can be seen with the unaided eye.

Projecting the Sun

The safest way to view sunspots or to watch the progress of an eclipse is to project the Sun onto a surface, such as through a pinhole in a box onto a piece of paper. Remove the lid from an elongated cardboard box—a shoe box is ideal—and paste white paper on the inside of one end to serve as a screen. In the center of the opposite end, cut a rough hole about an inch in diameter. Paste a sheet of aluminum foil over that hole, then make a circular hole in the foil with the tip of a sharp pencil. The bigger the hole, the brighter—and fuzzier—the image of the Sun will be; the smaller the hole, the sharper—and dimmer—the image. To use the box, aim the end with the hole toward the Sun until the Sun's image falls on the white paper. *Do not look at the Sun while doing this;* watch the paper until the image appears.

You can also project the Sun's image onto a sheet of paper using a lens. Do not use cemented lenses, such as those in binoculars, or the cement may melt. A simple lens with a long focal length (low power) works best. *Do not look through the lens;* look at the sheet of paper onto which you are projecting.

Viewing Eclipses *Never watch a solar eclipse through a telescope or binoculars or follow its progress with the naked eye.* View a solar eclipse only through a solar filter or by projecting the image (explained above). You can purchase a solar filter, good for looking at the Sun at any time, or make one by sandwiching at least two layers of fully exposed and developed black-and-white (not color) film between two pieces of glass and taping the edges. Welder's glasses (#13 or 14) will also work. Never look at the Sun, which should be just barely visible through the filter, for more than a few seconds at a time. During the totality phase of a total eclipse, it is completely safe to look at the Sun's corona with the naked eye, a camera, or binoculars, but be sure to stop looking when the Sun reappears or you might suffer eye damage. Partial and annular eclipses never reach totality, and cannot be viewed without a filter at any phase.

19

Observing the Moon

The best time to view the Moon is not at or near full moon, when the Sun's light falls most directly on the lunar surface and flattens its features, but before or after, when the angle of sunlight is more oblique, bringing out lunar features in high relief. Even 7-power binoculars show some detail on the Moon, and a small, low-power telescope is ideal. The Moon is too bright to view with larger (8″ to 14″ aperture) telescopes.

If you study the Moon over several nights you will see that each night the *terminator*, the dividing line between the illuminated part and the dark part of the Moon—and the best place to study lunar topography—is in a different place. As the terminator moves nightly, so do the shadows of lunar mountains and cliffs, creating a continually changing and fascinating spectacle. The terminator appears on the western limb (edge) of the waxing crescent just after new moon and moves eastward each night until full moon. After full moon the terminator reappears, and the Moon wanes until it disappears at new moon. The lunar maps that accompany the first- and last-quarter moon photographs on pages 148–151 of this guide identify many lunar features.

Key to the Color Plates

The following illustrations appear with each text description opposite the color plates. They offer a quick-reference guide to the subject covered.

The Sun in Our Sky

Midnight Sun

The Solar System

Star Comparisons

Solar Structure

The Solar Disk

Flares and Prominences

The Corona

Solar Eclipse

Annular Eclipse

Auroras

Lunar Phases

Lunar Eclipse

Lunar Occultation

Lunar Geography

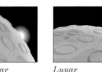

21

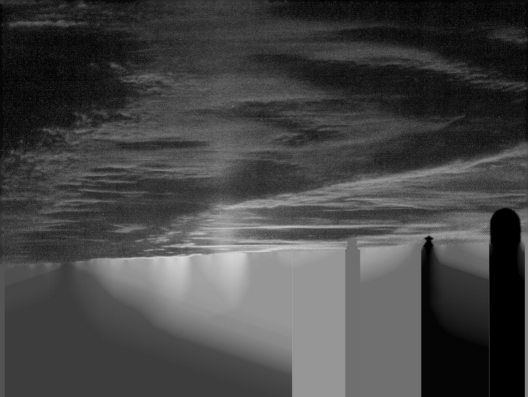

THE SUN

Sunrise
Wide-angle view from space shuttle Discovery

Our views of the Sun are always filtered through Earth's atmosphere. This view of the sunrise was photographed from aboard the space shuttle *Discovery,* Mission 39, in early May 1991, at an altitude of 155 km (96 miles). The bright blue and white band is caused by the scattering of light by molecules of atmospheric gases some 26 km (16 miles) above Earth's surface. The band follows the curvature of Earth. The dark area below the arc of light is the night side of Earth. The line between day (the blue and white band of light) and night is called the terminator. As Earth rotates the terminator moves across the planet, and the light of day moves with it. The blackness above the terminator in which the shuttle makes its orbit is outer space. Beyond Earth's atmosphere, which filters, scatters, and reflects the Sun's light, there are no "blue skies." Space is simply black.

Sunrise
Ground view

This view of the Sun near the horizon demonstrates some of the effects of Earth's atmosphere. When we look at an object near the horizon we are looking through many miles of lower atmosphere, which have a filtering effect. This is why the Sun looks less bright at such times than when it is directly overhead. It also gives us the redness of the sky at sunrise and sunset, caused by the preferential scattering of blue light waves by the atmosphere (so the light reaching us is on red wavelengths). The sphere of the Sun is markedly distorted here. Our atmosphere refracts (bends) light downward. Closer to the horizon, the bottom limb (edge) of the Sun passes through more air than does the upper limb, and the refraction is correspondingly greater. The "notches" in the limb of the Sun are caused by variations in atmospheric density, mainly temperature gradients. Just above the level of the ocean we see a partial "mirage," an image of the lower portion of the Sun's disk reflected on the sky. The Sun is also reflected on the ocean.

Midnight Sun
Baffin Island, Canada

We experience seasons, and variations in the length of day and night, because Earth's equator is tilted by 23½° to the plane of its orbit around the Sun. This tilt, called the obliquity, affects the amount of sunlight different locations receive over the course of a year. When the Northern Hemisphere is tipped toward the Sun, the Sun stays above the horizon for more than 12 hours a day, giving us the long, warm days of summer. Six months later, when the Southern Hemisphere points toward the Sun and the Northern tips away, the Sun is above the northern horizon for fewer than 12 hours a day, creating the Northern Hemisphere winter. This effect, barely noticeable near the equator, where days and nights are 12 hours long year round, increases in severity nearer to the poles. Within an imaginary circle 23½° from each pole (latitude 66½° N or S), the Sun never sets for part of the year; half a year later there is a corresponding time when the Sun never rises. When the Sun is up all night—the midnight sun—it is low on the horizon, giving us sunset colors, as seen here.

The Solar System
The Sun viewed from different planets

The Sun is our local star. While from Earth (150 million km/ 93 million miles away) it appears quite unlike any other object in the sky, from other, more distant planets the Sun is just a star, albeit an extremely bright one. An object's apparent size, that is, how large it appears in the sky, depends on its actual size and its distance. This illustration shows how the Sun appears from (left to right) Mercury, Earth, Jupiter, Saturn, and Uranus. From Mercury, the innermost planet, the Sun appears 2.58 times larger in diameter than it does from Earth and brings daytime temperatures up to 750°F (400°C). From Jupiter, an average distance of 778 million km (484 million miles) from the Sun, and Saturn, 1.427 billion km (887 million miles) distant, the Sun is a much less conspicuous presence, but still appears as a disk. From Uranus (2.87 billion km/1.783 billion miles) and beyond, the Sun appears to the unaided eye as an unresolved star, not at all as a disk. Sunlight does not flood the skies of the outermost planets; they experience eternal twilight, with the far-off Sun shining brighter than any other star.

The Solar System
The Sun and the planets

Our Sun is almost 10 times larger in diameter than Jupiter, the largest planet, which in turn is about 11 times larger than Earth. From left to right, this illustration shows, to scale, the Sun (in left margin), Mercury, Venus, Earth, Mars, the asteroid belt, Jupiter, Saturn, Uranus, Neptune, and Pluto. There are two types of planets: the small, terrestrial inner planets, and the four large, jovian (or gas giant) outer planets. (Puny, icy Pluto doesn't fit into either of these categories and has some characteristics of a comet.) The terrestrial planets, small, hard, and dense, have weak atmospheres. The large, primarily gaseous jovian planets are of low density, lack a hard surface, and have deep, massive atmospheres covered by intense radiation fields. These differences came about when the solar system was forming. The inner solar system, close to the Sun, was quite hot, and the gases that surrounded the embryonic planets there were boiled off by the heat. The planets, including Earth, were literally baked. The outer planets, far from the Sun's intense heat, were able to retain the gases that still surround their inner cores.

32

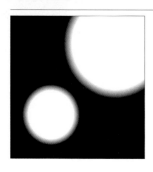

The Sun and Sirius A
Star comparisons

Sirius (also called the Dog Star), the alpha star in the constellation Canis Major, is a double star system (a pair of gravitationally bound stars). This illustration shows the Sun (left) and Sirius A, the brighter star of the system. The two immediate factors that govern energy flow (and thus brightness) from a star are how hot it is and how large it is. The surface temperature of a star is a measure of the star's power. Astronomers deduce the temperature of a star from its color and by interpreting the spectrum of the light it emits. Stars range from blue (hottest), through blue-white, white, yellow-white, yellow, and orange, to red (coolest). Sirius is a blue-white star, with a surface temperature of almost 10,000° Kelvin. The Sun is a yellow-white star, a moderate 5,800°K. Light flows in greater quantities from a large surface area than from a smaller one. Sirius is 1.75 times larger in diameter than the Sun, itself larger than most stars. Its size, temperature, and distance from Earth (only 8.7 light-years) combine to make Sirius the brightest star in the night sky. Side by side with the Sun, it would be 27 times more luminous.

34

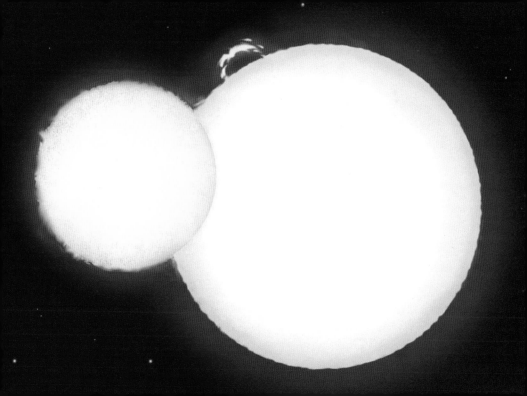

The Sun and Sirius B
Star comparisons

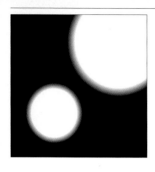

Sirius B (right) is 190 times smaller than its companion star, Sirius A. Turn-of-the-century astronomers studying the pair were befuddled by Sirius B. It was the same color as Sirius A, indicating that it had the same surface temperature, but its energy (light) output was 10,000 times fainter. They could deduce only that it was astonishingly small, and indeed, it has been determined that this star is only the size of Earth. This tiny, white-hot star was one of the first white dwarfs discovered. White dwarfs are the remains of stars after they have used up all possible energy generation from nuclear fusion. A moderate star like our Sun, for instance, after using up the hydrogen fuel in its core, will become a red giant and, at the end of that stage, shed its outer layers, leaving behind a white dwarf. Although they are very small, white dwarfs are extremely dense stars. Sirius B has the same mass as our Sun, even though it is 109 times smaller. A teaspoonful of the extremely dense material of a white dwarf would weigh several tons.

The Sun and Alpha Centauri ABC
Star comparisons

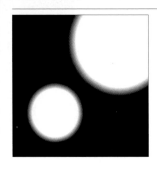

The triple star system known as alpha Centauri is the third-brightest star in the night sky and our Sun's nearest stellar neighbor, only 4.25 light-years away. Most stars in the universe have one or more companions; the Sun is an exception. Alpha Centauri A (top), the brightest of the three components, is almost identical to the Sun (the Sun is classified as type G2 V, alpha Centauri A as G1 V), but is 10 percent larger and more massive and somewhat older. The second-brightest star, alpha Centauri B (middle), is a type K1 V star, with a distinctly yellow coloration. It is about four-fifths the diameter of the Sun. These two stars orbit each other over an 80-year period, and lie about 3.440 billion km (2.130 billion miles) apart. Alpha Centauri C (bottom), known as Proxima Centauri because it is the closest star to our solar system, is a bit of a mystery to astronomers. A and B are thought to be 6 to 7 billion years old, but C seems to be a young, flaring dwarf star of spectral type M5 V. This suggests to some astronomers that this star, widely separated from A and B, is an unrelated interloper in the system.

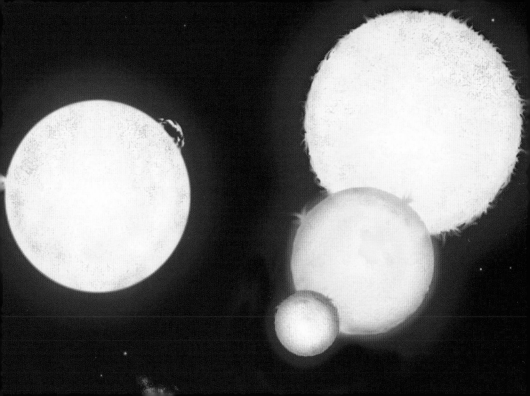

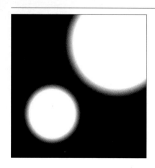

The Sun and Arcturus
Star comparisons

Arcturus (right), the alpha star in Boötes, is the brightest red giant in the night sky. Large, cool stars in the last major phase of their life cycle, red giants can range from yellow-orange to deep red. With a spectral type of K1.5 III, Arcturus is yellow-orange in color. It is about 25 times the size of the Sun, and has a surface temperature of 4,100°K. A red giant has depleted the hydrogen at its core, which in its main sequence phase it had been converting to energy by nuclear fusion. Energy production shifts to gravity compression of the core, hydrogen ("shell") fusion at the core's boundary with the lower, hydrogen-rich envelope, and later, helium fusion in the core. In red supergiants fusion reactions of other, heavier elements can occur, most notably carbon. These energy sources put out energy at a higher rate than hydrogen fusion at the core, expanding these stars to giant sizes and cooling—and thus reddening—their outermost atmosphere. This outer atmosphere will eventually be ejected into space, forming an escaping nebula, and the interior will compress to a tiny, dense white dwarf.

40

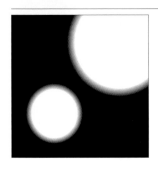

The Sun and Rigel
Star comparisons

Rigel (right), the beta star in Orion, is 1,500 light-years away and one of the brighter stars in the night sky. A rare hot supergiant of spectral type B8 Ia, Rigel is some 60 times larger than the Sun, with a temperature of about 13,400°K. Such stars are rare, in part because stars this massive—50 times the Sun's mass—are not made as often as lower-mass stars. Furthermore, such stars cannot maintain themselves for long. Massive stars squeeze themselves by their self-gravity more than lightweight stars do. This causes them to waste energy, burning their internal nuclear fires more rapidly. The rapid burning is the cause of their large sizes, heat, and luminosity. The blue-supergiant phase of a massive star is but a small fraction of its already brief lifespan. Rigel will be a blue supergiant for only about 1.5 million years, not long at all considering typical lifetimes of stars and durations of individual phases. The Sun, almost 4.6 billion years old, will be a main sequence star for another 5 billion years and then will spend another 3 billion in other phases before it runs out of fuel.

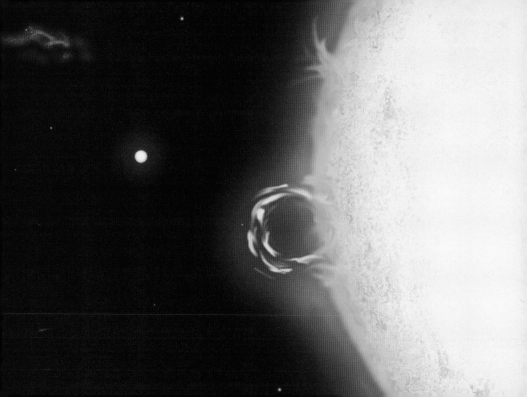

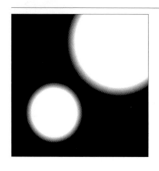

The Sun and Betelgeuse
Star comparisons

Betelgeuse (right) is the alpha star in Orion, marking
the eastern shoulder. It is variable in its light output,
going from as bright as magnitude 0.4 to as faint as 1.3.
The reason for its variability is hinted at by its spectral
class, M2 Iab. A red supergiant, Betelgeuse is in the final
stage of its active (generating energy by nuclear fusion)
lifetime. The outer atmosphere is so extended—to some
800 times the diameter of the Sun—that its surface
gravity is considerably weakened, allowing vast amounts
of matter to flow into space in the form of stellar wind.
During this time a supergiant star can lose a quantity of
mass equal to 5, 10, or more times the mass of our Sun.
(The quantity depends on the star's initial mass as well as
rotational factors and chemical composition.) Betelgeuse
is awash in surrounding nebulosity built up by its stellar
winds. It is one of three bright stars that astronomers
consider prime candidates to explode as supernovas. It
could happen any time in the next 100,000 years or so
and is sure to be a spectacle.

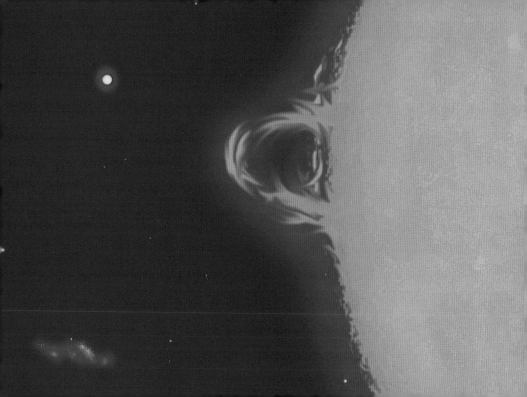

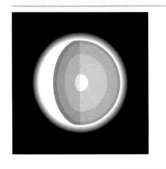

Solar Structure
Core to corona

A star has three general layers: the core, the envelope, and the atmosphere. The innermost region, the *core,* is the site of the nuclear fusion that generates the energy to sustain the star in all its immensity and luminous splendor. The Sun's core radius is about 10 percent of the total radius of the sphere. The role of the middle region, the envelope, is energy transport. As the second law of thermodynamics states, energy flows naturally from hotter areas to cooler areas. The energy generated within the core flows naturally outward, through the two layers in the envelope—the *radiative* and the *convective zones*—toward the surface, where it is emitted into space. The outer region of a star is its atmosphere, which consists of several layers. Relatively cool stars, like the Sun, may have an apparent surface. This lowermost atmospheric layer is called the *photosphere,* from which shines virtually all of the Sun's light. Above the photosphere is a thinner, dimmer, reddish layer called the *chromosphere,* and above that the extensive, pearly *corona,* reaching well out into space.

46

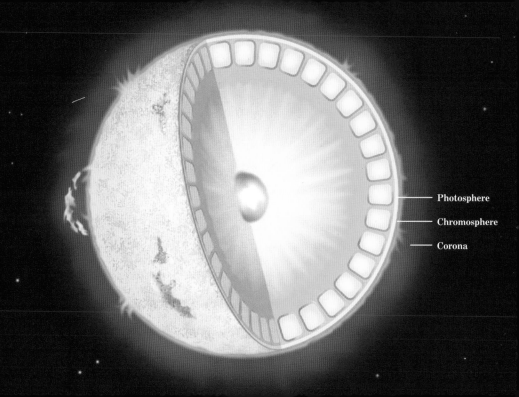

Photosphere

Chromosphere

Corona

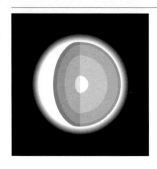

Solar Structure
The core and envelope

The Sun's energy production occurs only at its core, where from the weight of the overlying envelope, the Sun's plasma (ionized gases) experiences the greatest compression. The extremely high temperatures (some 15,000,000°K) and pressure (250 billion times that of Earth's atmosphere) enable protons (hydrogen nuclei) to fuse into helium, creating astonishing amounts of energy. Each second the Sun converts 5 million tons of hydrogen nuclei into energy. The energy produced in the hot core is compelled to reach the cooler surface (the photosphere), first by radiating through the radiative zone of the envelope, wherein lies most of the Sun's mass in the form of plasma. The plasma's free electrons are such strong scatterers of light that a given ray will take millions of years to reach the photosphere. Once the energy passes through the radiative zone it reaches the convective zone, where it is brought up to the surface by *convection cells*. The light, starting out as extremely high-energy gamma rays, is worn down on its journey to the lower-energy visible wavelengths we receive.

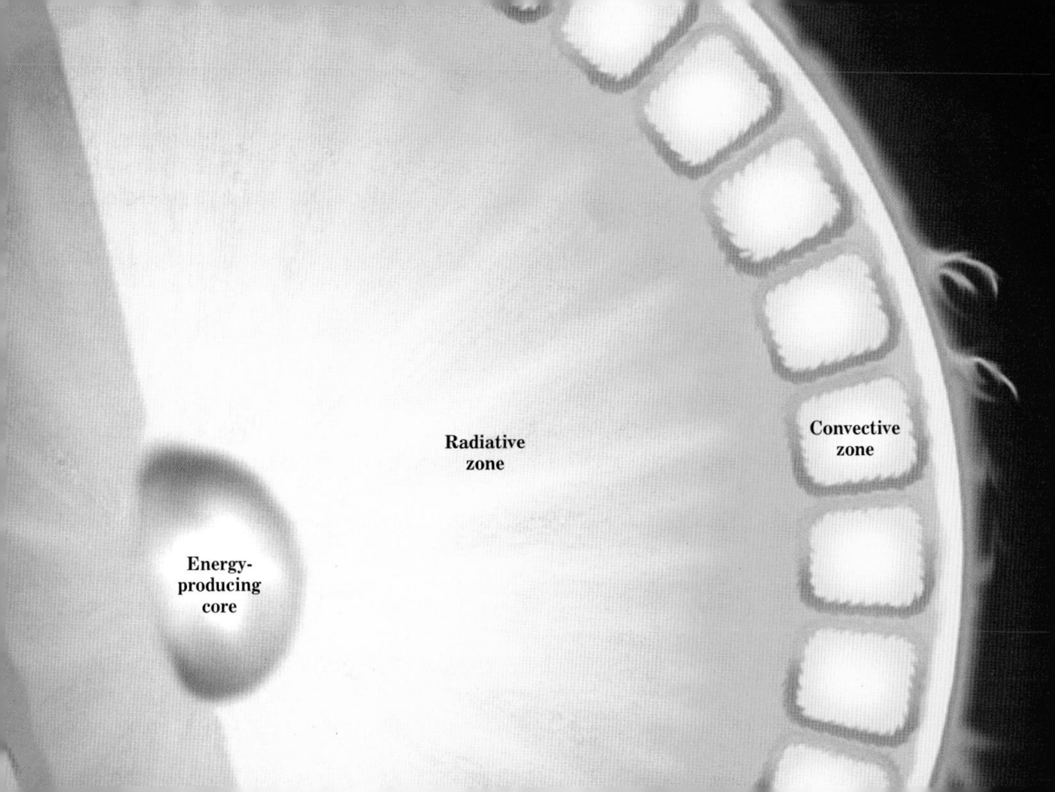

Radiative
zone

Convective
zone

Energy-
producing
core

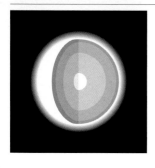

Solar Structure
Upper envelope and atmosphere

The apparent surface of the Sun is the photosphere layer of the atmosphere. This layer has the lowest average temperature, about 5,800°K, and appears opaque. The opacity ends sharply at a certain altitude in the Sun's atmosphere, giving the Sun its hard edge. The photosphere is the top of the convective zone, the outermost layer of the Sun's envelope, where convection cells transport heat up to the photosphere. The convection cells, also called *solar granulation cells,* give the Sun's surface a grainy appearance. Many cells are assembled in larger structures called *supergranules.* It is in the photosphere that sunspots associated with the Sun's magnetic field lines, are seen. The next layer, the chromosphere, is about 10,000 km (6,000 miles) thick. It is cooler, more tenuous (Earth's atmosphere is far denser), and radiates to a great extent at one particular wavelength (the hydrogen alpha line), visible as red light. Spikes of gases, called *spicules,* occur here. Finally, extending outward many millions of miles into space, is the corona. So thin it is essentially a vacuum, it is nevertheless extraordinarily hot, millions of degrees Kelvin

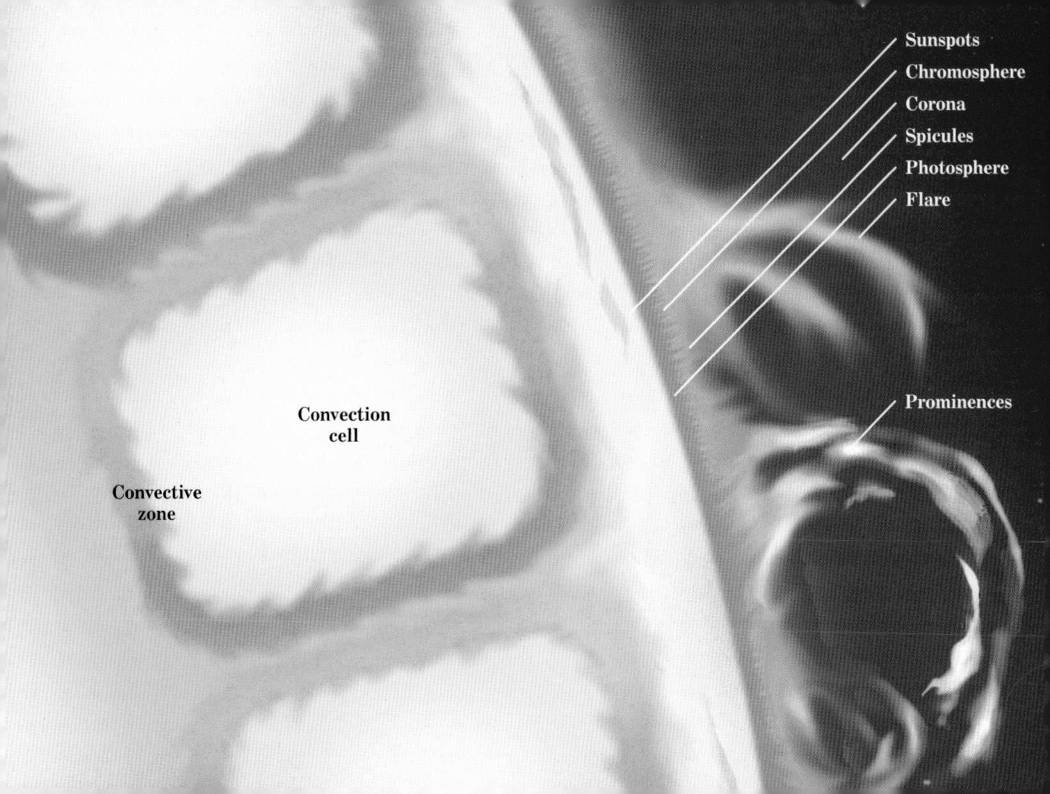

Sunspots
Chromosphere
Corona
Spicules
Photosphere
Flare

Prominences

Convection
cell

Convective
zone

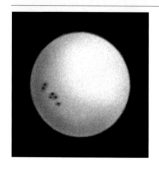

Solar Disk: Photosphere
White-light photograph

The Sun has no physical solid surface, but the opaque photosphere presents a visual surface. It is from the photosphere layer of the Sun, some 300 to 400 km (190 to 250 miles) thick, that most of the Sun's visible light comes. (For more on the photosphere, see the later section on eclipses.) Near the center of the disk are two large *sunspot* groups; several others trail off above and below. Sunspots appear darker than the rest of the Sun's "surface" because they are cooler and thus emit much less energy. The central spots in this image are only about 4,850°K, compared to the average surface temperature of 5,770°K. If not contrasted with the rest of the Sun's surface, these regions would appear to glow a very bright yellow-orange. Sunspots are formed in regions of intense magnetic activity, which represses the upward flow of hot gases. Sometimes bright regions known as *faculae* (literally, "little torches") can be seen on the solar surface. As these regions are slightly hotter than the surrounding photosphere, they glow more brightly.

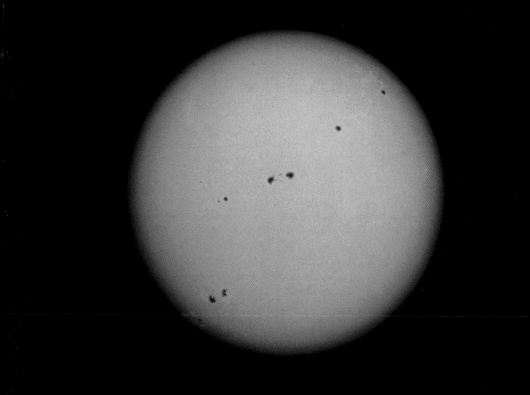

Solar Disk: Photosphere
Filtered (Hα) image

This photograph was taken with a filter that lets through only the red light of the hydrogen alpha (Hα) absorption line. Atoms of a given element emit or absorb light at only particular energies (wavelengths). Spectral lines result when an electron jumps from one energy level to another. At the Hα wavelength the Sun's photospheric gases are especially opaque, making it easier to image the regions that lie directly above the photosphere. The bright, cloud-like regions that appear yellow in this image are known as *plages*. Plage regions are indicators of higher-than-average magnetic activity and are usually, but not always, associated with visible sunspots. Plages that are visible in white light are called *faculae*. In this image the plage regions cross the solar disk in two bands above and below a line that corresponds to the Sun's equator. The two plage bands represent regions of opposite magnetic polarity. The edge (limb) of the Sun appears darker than the rest of the disk, because most light emerging from near the limb travels through more solar atmosphere to reach Earth.

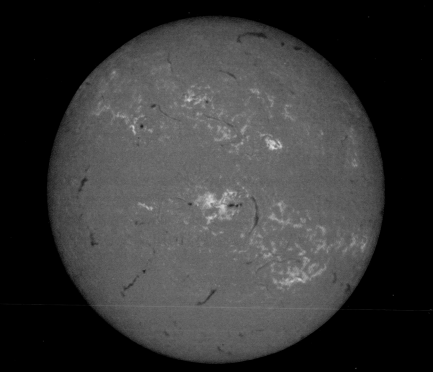

Solar Disk: Magnetic Field
Magnetogram

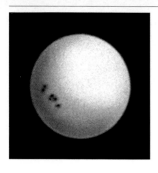

This magnetogram of the Sun indicates the polarity and intensity of the Sun's magnetic field. The false-color coding of this computer-generated image is as follows: Yellow indicates north (positive) polarity of the field; blue is south (negative) polarity. The Sun's equator runs horizontally across the center of the image. Strong magnetic fields are most apparent in two bands of activity—one north of the equator, the other south. Within these bands, the strongest magnetic fields are found near sunspots. Magnetograms can detect solar magnetic activity that is not visible to the eye. A magnetogram is not an actual "picture" of the Sun. Rather, it is a convenient way of assembling and displaying many thousands of measurements of magnetic field strength, orientation, and polarity across the field of view. Each measurement constitutes a single pixel in the final image.

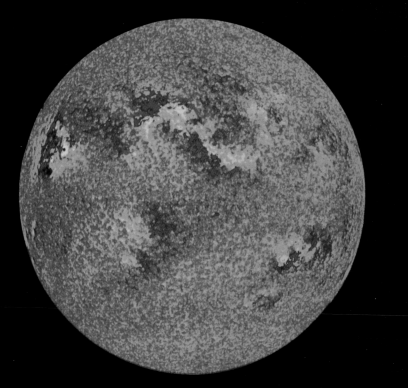

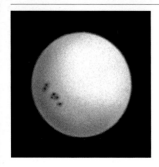

Solar Disk: Magnetic Activity
Magnetograms

These two magnetograms of the Sun show minimum (left) and maximum (right) solar magnetic activity levels. The quiet image, made on January 26, 1976, shows a more or less disorganized spatial distribution of local fields. (The horizontal stripes are irrelevant computer artifacts.) In the magnetogram made during an active period (January 3, 1978), magnetic activity is correlated with sunspot location and generally organized into two bands located symmetrically about the equator. The mean latitude of these bands changes systematically throughout a sunspot cycle, generally moving from the mid-latitudes toward the equator as time progresses. It has been known since the mid-19th century that the average number of sunspots varies within an 11-year period. We now know that the Sun's surface magnetic fields "flip" polarity with each new 11-year cycle (sunspots with a positive magnetic polarity switch to negative, and vice versa), making an overall 22-year solar magnetic activity cycle (MAC). At each 11-year peak of this cycle, sunspot numbers usually reach a maximum.

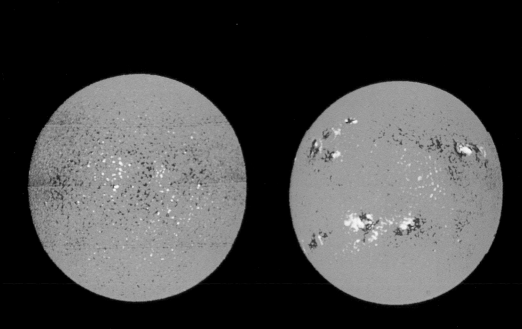

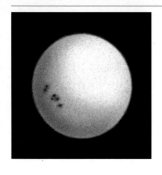

Solar Disk: Magnetic Activity
Magnetogram and heliogram

The image on the right is a heliogram (white-light picture of the Sun) obtained at the same time as the "active" magnetogram at left (also pictured in the preceding account). This pairing illustrates that visible sunspots are correlated with regions of high magnetic activity. Able to highlight regions where sunspots are either too small to be resolved or have too slight a temperature difference from the surrounding areas to be detected visually, magnetograms can serve as very sensitive early-warning sensors of where new sunspots eventually may appear. One of the reasons scientists study sunspots is to try to formulate a correlation between the number of sunspots and Earth's weather. During an extended period when there were almost no sunspots, from 1645 to 1715, there was a corresponding bout of cold weather in Europe (known as the Little Ice Age). In the past century there has been some correlation between the 22-year magnetic cycle and droughts in the central United States. Scientists have not yet been able to explain a connection between the Sun's magnetic activity and Earth's weather.

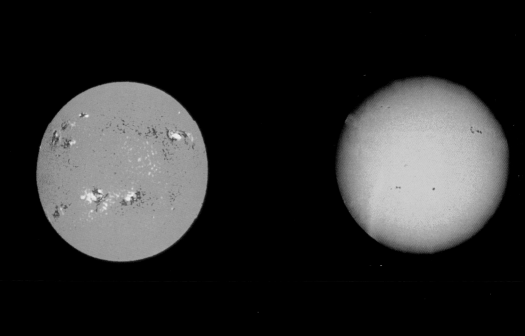

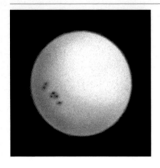

Solar Seismology
Computer simulation

Sound waves trapped within the Sun cause the surface to oscillate (vibrate) like a ringing bell. Roughly 10 million modes, or paths, of oscillation are known to exist. Some are radial, traveling from the center toward the surface (and vice versa), while others are transverse, moving along the surface. This computer-generated image highlights several of the most significant modes of oscillation. The blue-colored patches represent areas moving radially outward from the Sun's center; the red areas are those moving inward. Every few minutes, the direction of these motions reverses, with the red patches becoming blue and the blue patches red. These periodic oscillations occur in cycles of about five minutes. Observations of the precise period and strength of each mode of oscillation provide a wealth of information about the Sun's internal structure and dynamics: its temperature, pressure, density, composition, and perhaps even clues to its formation. In much the same way that seismologists have mapped the interior structure of Earth, astrophysicists are now trying to decode the Sun's hidden secrets with solar seismology.

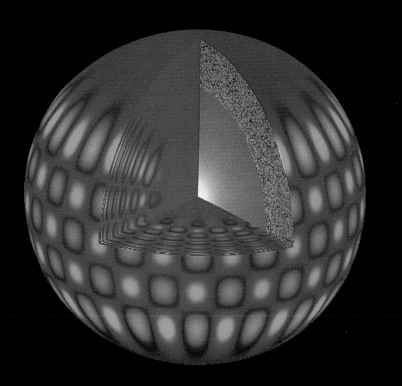

Solar Seismology
Computer simulation

This picture, another computer simulation of the oscillating surface of the Sun, shows approximately 100 modes of oscillation acting in concert to deform the surface of the Sun from a smooth spheroidal shape. In this image the surface displacements caused by the vibrations have been exaggerated, for emphasis, by approximately 1,000 times. The actual displacements each cover only a few kilometers on the Sun's enormous expanse, stretching nearly 1.4 million km (868,000 miles) in diameter. Although the actual displacements are so small, the speed of these oscillating parcels can be measured very accurately with an instrument called a spectrograph. As seen from Earth, rising parcels of solar plasma emit light at a slightly bluer wavelength than when they are falling, due to the Doppler effect, in which light waves change frequency depending on the relative motion of light source and observer. Each oscillation cycle—the time between successive risings—is on the order of five minutes.

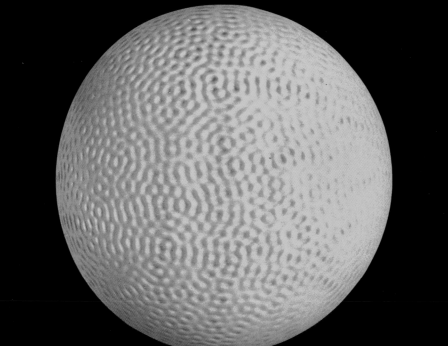

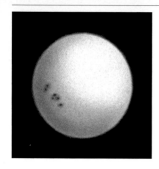

Sunspots and Solar Granulation Cells
White-light photograph

Sunspots, as seen in this close-up view (June 23, 1989), have a dark central region, called the *umbra* (Latin for "shade"), and a surrounding lighter region, the *penumbra* ("next to shade"). Reacting as iron filings do near a magnet, the penumbra's filamentary structure offers evidence that sunspots have a close connection to magnetic fields. The grainy appearance of the background is from *solar granulation* (or convection) *cells,* small heat-transporting regions 700 to 1,000 km (400 to 600 miles) wide that have lifetimes of a few minutes. As gases in the interior become heated they expand, becoming less dense and more buoyant, like bubbles. These cells transport solar energy, in the form of heated gases, from the hotter, lower regions to higher, cooler altitudes. When it rises to cooler regions, the gas fountains up, shedding its heat, becoming denser, and then sinking back down (the dark edges of each granule are the cooled gases). The centers of solar granules typically are 50 to 100°K hotter than the surrounding, sinking regions. Groups of granules form *supergranules.*

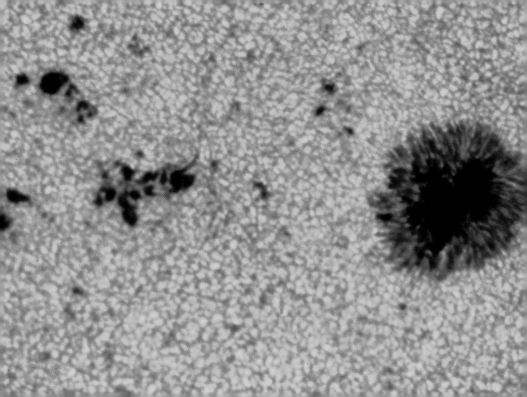

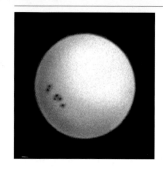

Sunspots
White-light photograph

These white-light images of an unusual spiral-shaped sunspot were obtained on February 19, 1982. Sunspots generally appear as dark, circular or irregularly shaped features. This unique spiral sunspot measured about six Earth diameters—some 80,000 km (50,000 miles) across—and persisted for about two days before breaking up into smaller spots. Sunspots tend to be transient features, appearing, intensifying, changing shape and location, and eventually disappearing over days or months. Well-developed sunspot groups such as this often have one or two large spots, with a train of smaller, less distinct spots trailing away from them. Using the laws of physics, scientists can predict how systems "should" behave—for example, which configurations are most stable and therefore most probable. Sunspots, however, are extremely changeable and unpredictable, and can form in innumerable configurations. Scientists have more luck predicting gross trends in sunspot activity, just as they can predict seasonal changes more easily than day-to-day weather.

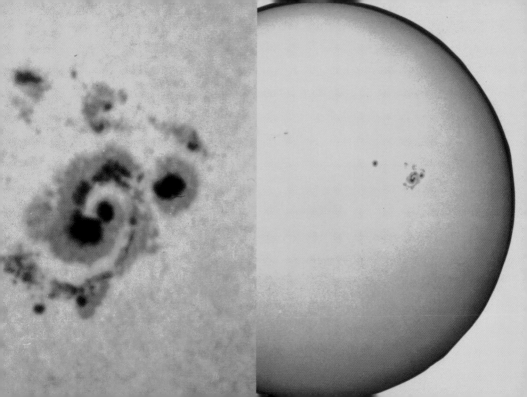

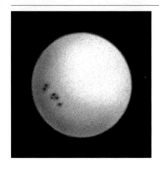

Sunspots
Magnetograms and white-light series

These sequences of images record the transit across the solar disk of a sunspot group during nine days in March 1989. This region of intense activity produced numerous powerful flares, composed of ions, electrons, and emissions of X rays and gamma rays. The sequence on the top was recorded in visible light; the images on the bottom are magnetograms. A magnetogram is a pictorial representation of magnetic field strength. The more intense a local magnetic field, the brighter (or darker) it appears on a magnetogram, depending on the magnetic polarity. Clearly this sunspot group is, as are all other such groups, a region of intense magnetic activity. The evolution of the sunspots over time is clear in both sequences. The shape changes systematically from day to day, even after accounting for projection effects on the apparent shape. It was by observing the progress of a sunspot group across the Sun's disk that Galileo was able to posit that the Sun makes one rotation a month. The Sun exhibits *differential rotation,* with its equatorial region turning more quickly than the poles.

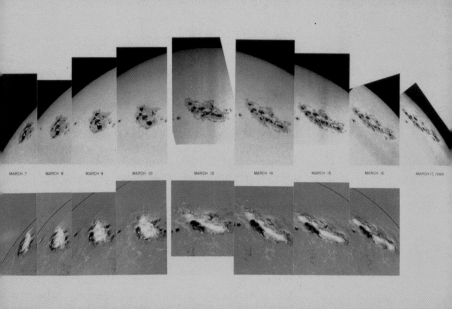

MARCH 7   MARCH 8   MARCH 9   MARCH 10   MARCH 13   MARCH 14   MARCH 15   MARCH 16   MARCH 17, 1969

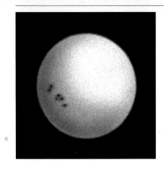

Sunspots
White-light and magnetic field images

The natural-light photograph at the right shows a close-up photograph of a complex sunspot region. The image on the left is a spectrogram (an image of a spectrum), which illustrates what happens to a light source when it is affected by a strong magnetic field. The vertical black line through the sunspot indicates the area that was imaged in the spectrogram. When a spectrograph focuses on a sunspot or other region with an intense magnetic field, it shows more than the normal solar spectrum—some of the spectral lines have been split in three (this is called the Zeeman effect). In this image of the sunspot's dark region, a spectral line of iron "splits" into three lines. This line actually is a composite resulting from three different atomic transitions of nearly the same energy. The space between the individual lines is proportional to the intensity of the applied magnetic field. This image illustrates a field strength of 4,130 gauss (a unit of magnetic flux density). Compare this to the average Earth magnetic field of about half a gauss. Vertical lines in the spectrogram are due to absorptions by different elements in the solar atmosphere.

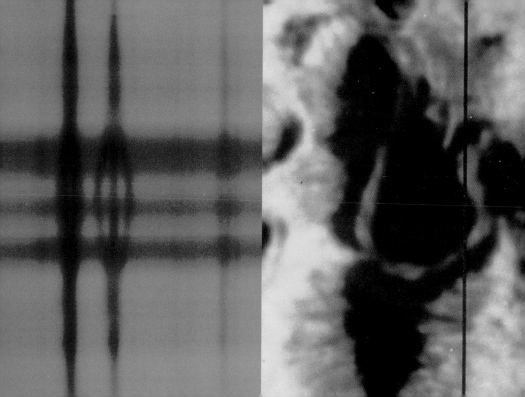

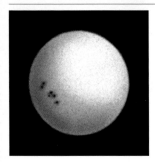

Sunspots
Magnetogram, natural-light, and false-color images

This triptych presents three different types of images of a sunspot group near the limb (edge) of the Sun made on February 13, 1978. This is a typical bipolar sunspot group—the magnetic field lines exit the photosphere through one sunspot and reenter through the other. At left is a magnetogram with false-color coding. Yellow indicates north polarity; blue indicates south. The pinkish area is a region of particularly high magnetic field strength. The middle image is a natural-light photo of the same region. The right frame, with false colors representing different radial velocities, shows the component of the velocity field along our line of sight. In this image, blue shows motion away from us, yellow toward our line of sight. Note that the regions of highest velocity (whitish-yellow) correspond to the regions of most intense magnetic activity. Charged plasma (ions and electrons) tends to follow magnetic field lines, spinning around them at high speed and traveling along them in a tightly wound spiral trajectory.

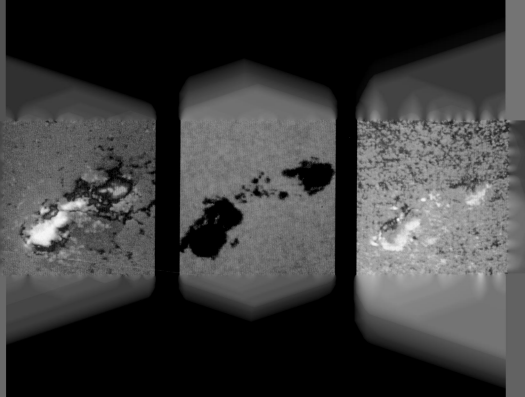

Sunspots
Magnetogram

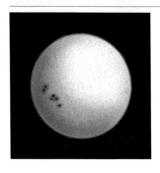

This magnetogram is a close-up of an active region on the Sun on July 4, 1974, with false-color coding used to indicate north polarity (yellow) and south polarity (blue) of the field. In sunspots, regions of opposing polarity tend to be paired; much as an electrical circuit needs positive and negative poles, so does a dipole magnetic circuit. For this reason, sunspots or groups of sunspots very often are seen in pairs rather than singly. Sunspot pairs usually align themselves east to west, in a leading-trailing fashion, as the Sun rotates eastward. The magnetic polarity for all such pairs is identical throughout an 11-year sunspot cycle. At the start of the next cycle the magnetic polarity switches, and the hemisphere that had a north magnetic polarity in the leading sunspots in sunspot pairs switches to south polarity for its leading spots. Two consecutive sunspot cycles complete a 22-year magnetic activity cycle (MAC).

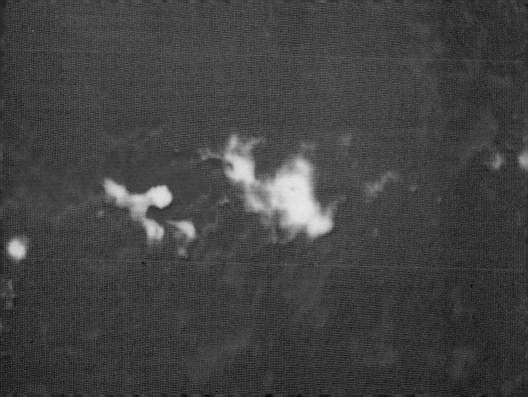

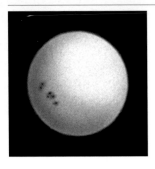

Spicules
Filtered (Hα) image

Jet-like spikes of cool gas known as *spicules* rise vertically from between groups of supergranules on the solar surface. When viewed from the side (near the limb, or edge, of the Sun), they have the appearance of a forest or a series of picket fences. Each "picket fence" surrounds a supergranule, an area about 30,000 km (18,600 miles) in diameter composed of a few dozen to a few hundred individual convection cells, also called granules. Spicules may seem to be small, incidental features when compared to the entire solar disk, but during their brief lives— lasting only about 10 minutes—spicules rise to heights of 5,000 to 10,000 km (3,000 to 6,000 miles) above the photosphere. Gas in spicules rises at a speed of about 30 km (19 miles) per second. At any one time there are about 300,000 spicules on the solar surface. Clear images of spicules show up best in hydrogen alpha (Hα) images of the Sun, such as this one.

Solar Flare
Ionized helium ultraviolet image

One of the most spectacular solar flares ever recorded is shown in this photograph made aboard *Skylab* on December 19, 1973. This image was made not in visible light but in the extreme ultraviolet light of ionized helium. The bottoms of the arch span more than 588,000 km (365,000 miles) across the solar surface. The material is extending 405,000 km (250,000 miles) into space, about the distance from Earth to the Moon. At this stage in its development the flare has the form of a prominence but is much larger, and the material is blasting outward, not cascading downward. Also of interest in this photograph is the Sun's surface. The poles (at the top and bottom of the image) appear darker than the rest of the solar disk and show a decrease in the supergranulation (the speckled pattern) that covers the Sun's surface. Two bands of bright (more active) regions straddle the equator. The bottom band is more obvious to the eye. To find the location of the topmost band, look for the bright spot on the western (right) edge of the Sun. (The flare straddles the active region on the eastern limb.)

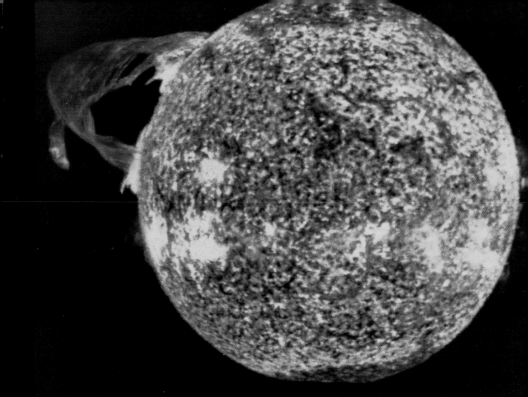

Solar Flare
Filtered (Hα) image

In this image of an active region near the limb of the Sun, flame-like features called *solar flares* rise high above the limb. A solar flare is a relatively rapid and energetic eruption that reaches peak brightness about 10 minutes after its onset. It can take between 10 minutes and several hours to fade away. Manifestations of intense, transient magnetic activity, flares occur most frequently near complex sunspot groups and during periods when many sunspots exist. Flares release tremendous amounts of energy in a relatively short time: Ejected material can reach speeds of 1,000 km (600 miles) per second. In the ultraviolet region of the spectrum, a modestly sized flare can outshine the rest of the Sun. Flares can emit energetic X rays and gamma rays, which can pose serious threats to spacecraft. Earth's atmosphere shields us from most of this harmful radiation. However, charged particles that stream from the Sun with a flare eruption can disrupt Earth's ionosphere, interfering with radio communications. Geomagnetic storms brought on by flares can trigger auroral displays in our skies.

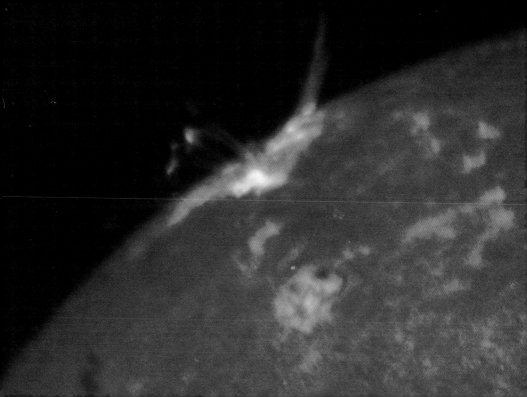

Solar Flare
Filtered (Hα) image

This solar flare has the appearance of another type of limb activity, a prominence. Although flares are generally more violent, and more transient, eruptions, it is not always easy to distinguish the two in still photographs. Unlike flares, most prominences can remain stable for periods ranging from hours to days, and they typically reach several tens of thousands of kilometers in altitude. Prominences appear to be material ejected from the Sun, as flares are, but time-lapse photography in Hα light shows that more often they are cool, dense regions of the Sun's outer atmosphere (the corona) that are moving downward along magnetic field lines. As atoms of this relatively cool material capture free electrons, they emit light. Prominences often lie near the boundaries of regions possessing opposite magnetic polarity. Sudden changes in magnetic fields (called transients) can result in flares as well as more violent and shorter-lived eruptive prominences that span distances of more than 1 million km (620,000 miles).

Prominences: After Solar Flare Eruption
Filtered (Hα) image

Obtained over an eight-hour interval in 1985, this series
of images shows the progress (left to right) of a solar
flare eruption. During the eruption, magnetic field lines
snapped, much as an overstressed rubber band will break
(though not so completely). Glowing plasma, which tends
to move along magnetic field lines, was shot out into
interplanetary space. Magnetic field lines do not "like" to
have free ends; their broken parts attract one another to
form continuous loops. These photographs document the
healing process of the broken field lines: Over a period of
a few hours, many of the breaks re-form into loops, called
prominences. Although we cannot see the actual magnetic
field lines, their positions are traced by the arcs of plasma
that cling to the lines as they move out into space. While
a several-hour healing period may seem like a long time,
this process actually is very rapid, considering the large
distances (many thousands of kilometers) involved.

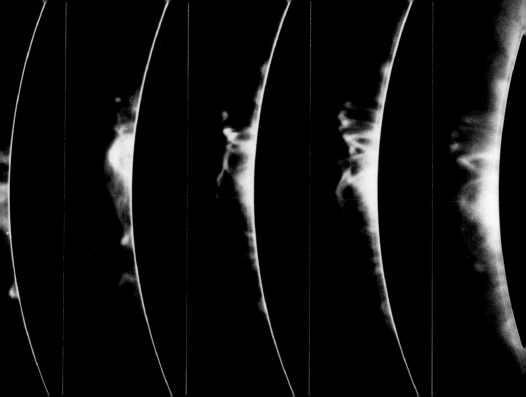

Prominence: Eruptive Type
Filtered (Hα) image

This eruptive solar prominence, which occurred on June 20, 1989, is seen in the red light of Hα. An eruptive prominence can lift material from the surface at speeds approaching 700 km (435 miles) per second, fast enough for the material to escape into interplanetary space. Hydrogen gas in the lower part of this loop is falling inward toward the Sun. Prominences often take on arch- or loop-shaped geometries, as the plasma tends to follow magnetic field lines back to the photosphere. The most powerful prominences can visibly extend out to a distance equivalent to several solar radii. Rarer but more powerful than eruptive prominences are the so-called surge prominences, in which ejection velocities can be as much as double those of the eruptive type of prominence. These enormous eruptions from the Sun, along with weaker but more frequent eruptions, will discourage any future human exploration of the Sun's vicinity, and probably even of Mercury as well. Robotic spacecraft that are sufficiently resistant to heat and particle radiation will have to do the job for us.

88

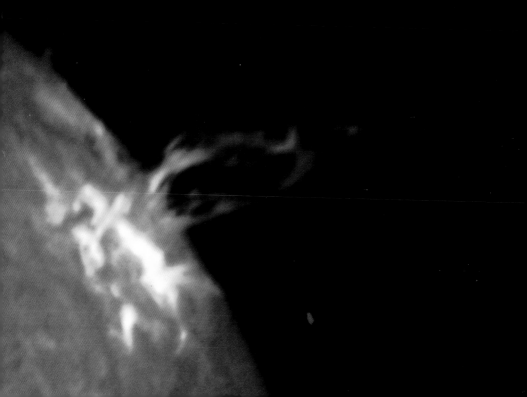

Prominence: Quiescent Type
False-color image

This classic multiple-arch prominence, photographed in the mid-1960s, is a single frame from a time-lapse movie of the event. In the movie, material—mostly neutral and ionized hydrogen, the rest helium—can be seen circulating along the arches, first emerging from the photosphere at an active (sunspot) region, rising high above the surface, and returning along the arches to a nearby active region. These types of eruptions, called *quiescent prominences*, can last from a few days to a few months. Less energetic than solar flares, prominences expand outward and then fall back to the photosphere. Flares are more eruptive, expelling much matter and high-energy light wavelengths far into space. An instrument called a coronagraph, a telescope with a special "occulting mask" that is used to block out the bright disk of the Sun, was used for this photograph. Before the invention of the coronagraph, scientists had to wait for solar eclipses, during which our Moon served as the occulting mask, to study the Sun's outer atmosphere.

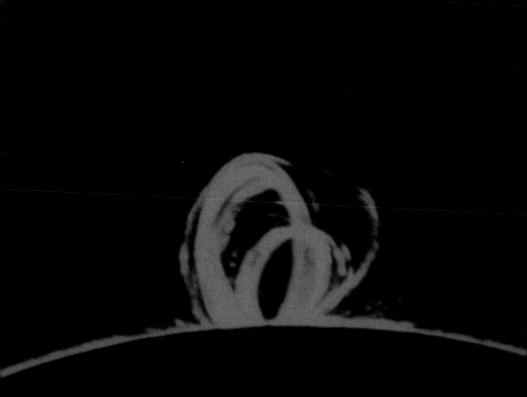

Corona
False-color image from Skylab

Skylab, the first U.S. space station, launched in May 1973, was equipped with a coronagraph, an instrument that blocks out the Sun's disk so the corona can be studied. The corona (crown), the Sun's tenuous outer atmosphere, is much hotter than the photosphere, with a typical temperature of around 2,000,000°K. Despite these extremely high temperatures, the corona is relatively dim because of its very low density (the air around us is many times denser). In this false-color image of the corona taken by *Skylab*, different colors distinguish different levels of brightness. Two roughly symmetrical regions of hot, rarefied coronal gases extend millions of miles from the Sun's equatorial surface. The bulge on the left resulted from a large flare. The distinctive distribution is caused by the Sun's magnetic field lines, along which the coronal material flows. Streamers of coronal gases have been recorded extending into space a distance equivalent to 20 solar radii. *Skylab* made eight months of coronal observations, enabling scientists to study changes in the corona over time.

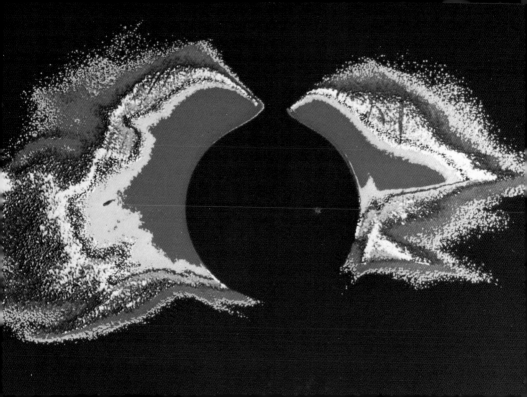

Coronal Holes
X-ray view from Skylab

The Solar Telescope of the U.S. *Skylab* mission acquired this X-ray image of the Sun during the 1970s. Earth's surface is shielded from X rays by its atmosphere, so we must go into space for data emitted at these short, energetic wavelengths. Images such as this one led astronomers to the discovery of "holes" in the inner corona, indicated in this image by the dark areas. The large, bright areas visible here, indicative of extremely hot temperatures, lie over active regions of the Sun's surface, as can be seen from comparisons to magnetograms made at about the same time. These active regions tend to be restricted to the Sun's mid- to lower latitudes. At a dark, cooler coronal hole, the Sun's magnetic field lines extend out into space, allowing plasma (ions and electrons) which tends to spiral along magnetic fields in a helical fashion, to escape in all directions from the Sun in the form of solar wind. Planetary magnetic fields deflect much of the solar wind but focus some down onto the magnetic poles. This is the source of auroral displays in the skies of Earth's polar regions.

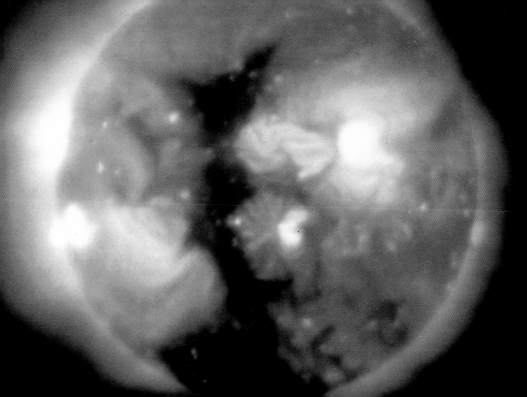

Coronal Holes
Infrared image

In this image the solar disk is viewed in the near-infrared light of helium at a wavelength that is just about twice as long as that to which our eyes are most sensitive. This helium line is very useful for filtered images of the hot corona, as helium is the second most abundant element in the Sun after hydrogen. This helium wavelength is produced at much higher temperatures than the Hα line is, which is why the helium line is a very good tracer of coronal activity. Coronal holes are regions where the Sun' magnetic field lines are "disconnected." The north and south poles of the Sun have permanent coronal holes, but those seen at lower latitudes tend to be more transient in nature, lasting for periods ranging from a few to several solar rotations. The energetic solar wind, a stream of plasma, charged atoms, and electrons, exits mainly through coronal holes into the interplanetary medium.

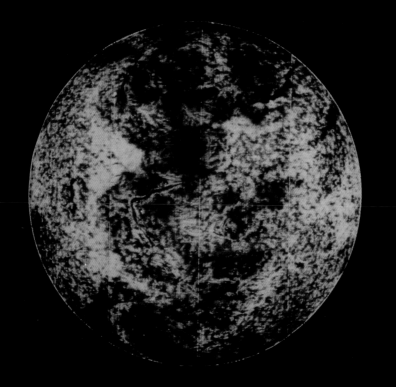

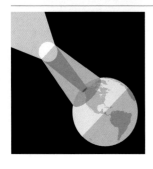

Solar Eclipse
Ground view

This wide-angle view of the total solar eclipse of July 11, 1991, looks over the telescopes of Mauna Kea, Hawaii. The light from the photosphere, the visible "surface" of the Sun, has been cut off by the intervening new moon, allowing the much dimmer light of the hot, rarefied gases of the corona to be visible. The corona is pearly or silvery in color and filamentary in structure. During a total solar eclipse, at the phase called *totality* (when the Moon completely masks the Sun's disk) the corona provides lighting conditions somewhere between those of deep twilight and a night with a full moon. The unusually large and brilliant corona of this eclipse cast distinct shadows on the ground. Totality lasted almost 7 minutes—close to the maximum possible and not to be exceeded until the year 2132. The *path of totality*—the area on Earth over which the Moon's shadow swept and where the total eclipse could be seen—moved across Hawaii, through Mexico, and into South America. Surrounding areas saw a partial eclipse, during which the Sun was never completely covered.

Solar Eclipse
Time-sequence photograph

This striking time-sequence photograph of the July 11, 1991, solar eclipse was taken above a cathedral in La Paz, Mexico. During a solar eclipse the *umbra* of the Moon's shadow reaches Earth as a fairly small area, a maximum of only 250 km (160 miles) wide. Totality can be seen only within the narrow geographical area in the umbral shadow. With the rotation of Earth, the shadow traces a path along Earth's surface; this is called the *path of totality.* If you are in the *penumbra*, a much lighter outer shadow, you will see a partial eclipse. A solar eclipse has four phases: *first contact,* when the Moon's shadow first touches the edge of the Sun; *second contact,* when the Moon completely covers the Sun (also called totality); *third contact,* when the Moon begins to uncover the Sun; and *fourth contact,* when the Moon's shadow is no longer touching the Sun. There are at least two solar eclipses each year, but because the path of totality is so small, most of us do not get to witness totality. See the listing of upcoming solar eclipses in the appendices if you would like to plan a trip to see this awesome celestial event.

100

Solar Eclipse: Annular
Time-sequence photograph

During total solar eclipses, along the path of totality the Moon's disk completely covers that of the Sun. In many eclipses it doesn't, and the result is an *annular eclipse,* such as the one of May 10, 1994, shown here, in which an annulus (ring) of sunlight remains visible. Although the Moon's actual size (3,476 km/2,160 miles in diameter) is much smaller than the Sun's (about 1,392,000 km/865,00 miles in diameter), coincidentally the distances of the Sun and the Moon from Earth have the same ratio as do their sizes. Therefore, the two objects appear to be the same size in the sky. The Moon revolves around our planet in a elliptical path, so that it is roughly 40,000 km (25,000 miles) farther from Earth when at its farthest point (known as *apogee*) than when at its closest point (*perigee*) When the Moon is near apogee, it is far enough away that its angular size is noticeably smaller than that of the Sun During solar eclipses that occur at this time, the Moon does not completely block the disk of the Sun, allowing observers on Earth to see a ring of photosphere around the Moon's shadow.

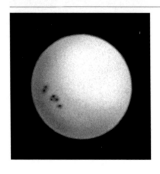

Solar Eclipse: Partial
Features of the photosphere

In this photograph, taken during a partial solar eclipse, features of the Sun's photosphere are visible. Composed entirely of hot ionized gases (plasma), the Sun has no physical surface, but the photosphere (some 300 to 400 km/190 to 250 miles thick) has the right temperature and pressures to appear opaque. Like a billowy cumulus cloud in Earth's skies, it presents a distinct visual surface and gives the Sun its clearly defined edges. This layer shields the Sun's interior from view and is the source of virtually all the visible light we see on Earth. In this imag the edge of the Sun, called the limb, appears darkened because most of the light from the limb travels a much longer path through the solar atmosphere than the light emitted from nearer the center of the solar disk. The photosphere has a slightly grainy or speckled appearance caused by pockets of hot gas that circulate through the upper layers of the Sun. Called granules, these convection cells bring hot, bright gas to the surface, where it cools and sinks back into the interior. Several dark sunspots ar visible, particularly near the limb.

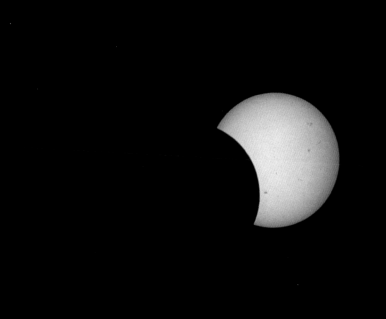

Solar Eclipse
Features of the chromosphere

Above the photosphere, the visible "surface" of the Sun, are two additional layers of gas known collectively as the solar atmosphere. Immediately adjacent to the photosphere is the chromosphere, a thin layer—about 6,000 km (3,700 miles) thick—filled with jets and loops of reddish gas. The distinctive red color, which gives the chromosphere its name (*chrom-* means color), is caused by the emission of a specific wavelength of light from hydrogen gas (the Hα absorption line). Above the chromosphere is the corona, pearly or silvery in color. This photograph shows two reddish prominences, huge eruptions of chromospheric gas, extending into the corona on either side of the Sun. Generally associated with sunspots, prominences often display an arched shape as the erupted gas flows along the loop of a contorted magnetic field line. Some prominences shoot outward in a matter of hours, while others, called quiescent prominences, hang suspended above the photosphere for weeks or even months. The small jets of gas, called spicules, that surround the photosphere's supergranules also extend into the chromosphere layer.

106

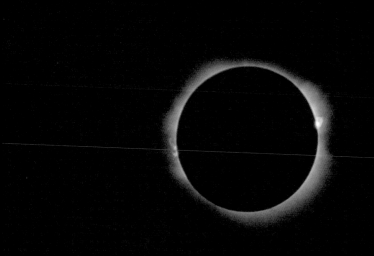

Solar Eclipse
Features of the corona

Above the chromosphere, the temperature of the solar atmosphere rises abruptly in just a few dozen kilometers, from roughly 5,000 to 10,000°K at the top of the chromosphere to approximately 500,000°K at the base of the corona. The characteristic pearly color of coronal light results from the scattering of light from the photosphere by free electrons (subatomic particles) in the hot coronal gas. The corona, like the air in a dusty room, is mostly transparent and scatters only a small fraction of the photospheric light. The size and shape of the corona reflect the state of the Sun's magnetic field. During a period of low sunspot activity, when the magnetic field is fairly orderly, the corona appears smaller, regular, and symmetric, with delicate feathery plumes streaming from the Sun's polar regions. During a period of high sunspot activity, when the magnetic field is relatively contorted, the inner corona brightens and its shape is much more irregular, with large streamers extending far into space.

108

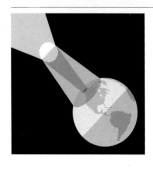

Solar Eclipse
Baily's beads

As the Moon passes in front of the Sun during a solar eclipse, the disk of the Sun shrinks to a thin crescent of light. The encroaching limb (edge) of the Moon is not smooth, but is made irregular by the mountains, valleys, and craters on the lunar surface. During the final seconds before totality, the last vestiges of the Sun's photosphere are seen as a series of brilliant spots of light peeking through the valleys along the lunar limb. These points of light are known as *Baily's beads.* Usually the Sun and the Moon appear to be about the same size in the sky. However, the Moon's orbit around Earth is not circular but elliptical, and when the Moon is close to Earth, its apparent size is slightly larger than the Sun's. This reduces the narrowing solar crescent as totality approaches; under these conditions, the number of Baily's beads is also reduced. In this photograph two bright Baily's beads are visible, as is a reddish prominence a huge eruption of chromospheric gas. At the end of totality, as the Sun emerges from behind the Moon's shadow, Baily's beads may reappear.

110

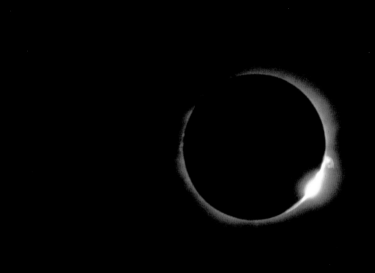

Solar Eclipse
Diamond ring

During the last moments in a solar eclipse before the Moon completely covers the surface of the Sun, a single spot of photospheric light shines through a gap on the Moon's edge, or limb. This single Baily's bead appears as a brilliant gem set on a band of ghostly, subdued coronal light, creating what is known as the *diamond ring effect.* This occurs only briefly and must be captured by photographers very quickly. As the jewel-like spot of light disappears behind the advancing Moon, the brilliant red chromosphere, the thin lower layer of the solar atmosphere, may be visible for an instant before it, too, is eclipsed and the full glory of the corona is revealed. Totality, during which the Sun's photosphere is totally hidden from view and the corona is fully visible, lasts from a few seconds to more than seven minutes, depending on the position of the observer and the distance of the Moon from Earth. Following totality, the Sun peeks out from the Moon's limb and a second diamond ring may appear.

Rainbow
Optical phenomenon

Sunlight and water bring us the ephemeral beauty of rainbows. When light passes through a water droplet, it is refracted (bent) inside the droplet, which functions as a prism. When this refracted light reflects once off the inside of the droplets, a bright *primary rainbow* results. Its colors range from violet on the interior edge through blue, green, yellow, and orange to red on the outer edge. When the refracted sunlight is reflected twice in the water droplets, a fainter *secondary rainbow* appears, with the color sequence reversed. The primary rainbow is always 42° away from the antisolar point (the direction exactly opposite the Sun), and the secondary rainbow is 10° higher. The tallest and longest rainbows occur when the Sun is near the horizon. Rainbows can't appear when the Sun is too high. Between the primary and secondary rainbows in this photograph is a region known as *Alexander's dark band.* The way light leaves a water droplet adds light to the inside of the primary rainbow and the outside of the secondary rainbow, causing the region between the two to appear dark in contrast.

114

Parhelion
Optical phenomenon

The rainbow-like patch of light visible in this photograph of the Alaskan wilderness is a parhelion (also called a *sun dog* or *mock sun*). The side facing the Sun is red, with a reasonably well-defined edge. A middle band of yellow grades into the bluish-white outer region, which is stretched out into a blurry tail that points away from the Sun. Parhelia always appear to the right and left of the Sun at the same distance above the ground, although sometimes only one parhelion is visible. They are often, but not always, associated with halos around the Sun. Parhelia occur when ice crystals (rather than water droplets, which produce rainbows) refract the sunlight in their interiors to create the spectrum of colors. Ice crystals come in a variety of sizes and shapes, including six-sided plates; six-sided, flat-topped pillars; six-sided, pointed rockets; and various combinations of plates and pillars. Parhelia occur when all the ice crystals refracting the light are roughly the same size and orientation. As the ice crystals are never perfectly aligned, parhelia are fuzzy, with blurred edges.

116

Sun Halo
Optical phenomenon

This photograph captures a halo around the Sun. The inner edge of the halo is red and fairly sharp, while the outer edge is bluish-white and ill-defined. A sun halo is produced by refraction (bending) of sunlight by ice crystals in high, wispy cirrus clouds, in a process similar to those that produce parhelia and rainbows. The colors of the halo are most vivid when the cirrus clouds form a uniform haze layer. Unlike the colors of a rainbow or a parhelion, those of a halo are muted because the ice crystals refracting the sunlight have a variety of sizes, shapes, and orientations. Often, when clouds are unevenly distributed, the halo is simply pale white, with no color at all. Most commonly, a halo is located 22° away from the Sun (approximately the width from little finger to thumb when your hand is held up at arm's length with fingers spread). Sometimes a second halo can be seen 46° away from the Sun. Rarely, this larger halo may be seen alone. Halos are often accompanied by parhelia. If the Sun is near the horizon, the parhelia will be superimposed on the halo. When the Sun is higher in the sky, the parhelia will be farther out.

118

Sun Pillar
Optical phenomenon

This photograph shows a column of light, known as a sun pillar, rising upward from the Sun, which has just set below the horizon. Sun pillars are caused by light reflecting off the surfaces of ice crystals of two specific shapes—a six-sided flat plate and a six-sided column—whose widest dimension is oriented nearly horizontally. The closer to horizontal the crystals are, the shorter, narrower, and more sharply defined the sun pillar. Pillars caused by plate-shaped ice crystals extend above and below the Sun, but not through it, when the Sun is near or beneath the horizon. Pillars caused by column-shaped ice crystals are short and pass through the Sun. Sun pillars reflect the color of the Sun, and as pillars are usually associated with the rising or setting Sun, they are often orange or red. Sun pillars have been observed on rare occasions at the same time as a sun halo and parhelia. The result is an eerie, luminous cross centered on the Sun, suspended in the sky. Pillars of light may also be seen extending from the Moon and even from streetlamps on nights when ice crystals are in the air.

120

Green Flash
Optical phenomenon

On rare occasions, in a clear, haze-free sky with a low, straight horizon, a brilliant flash of emerald green light occurs just before the Sun sinks. Earth's atmosphere refracts light in the same manner that a prism does, although the effect is very slight. Near the horizon, where refraction is greatest, the image of the Sun separates into slightly offset multiple images in this order: red, orange, yellow, green, blue, violet. Where the images overlap, the Sun appears normal. The uppermost images, blue and violet, are not usually visible, as light of these colors is strongly scattered by air. Of those remaining, green is the most easily discerned by the human eye and may be glimpsed briefly as a thin green rim on the top of the setting Sun. When sunlight is refracted by an inversion layer (in which temperature increases rather than decreases with altitude), an image from the lower portion of the Sun is superimposed over an upper segment, isolating a piece of the Sun's rim above the main disk (as seen in this photograph where the spikes appear). This small segment may turn green just before the Sun sets.

Aurora
Ground view

The eerie, silent beauty of an auroral display is an awesome sight. Auroras result when charged particles (ions and electrons) streaming from the Sun encounter Earth's magnetic field, generating enormous electrical currents that flow along the magnetic field lines and enter Earth's atmosphere at the geomagnetic poles, which lie near the geographic north and south poles. Charged particles accelerated by these currents collide with gases in the upper atmosphere, causing those gases to fluoresce, in the same way that gases in the tube of a fluorescent lamp glow when the current is turned on. The fluorescing gases produce a colorful variety of shimmering arcs, rays, and curtains of light. Sometimes, as in this photograph, the aurora appears as a series of vertical rays of light. The colors of an aurora depend on the composition and altitude of the gases involved. Nitrogen, the most abundant gas in Earth's atmosphere, generally produces shades of blue and violet. Oxygen between 110 and 240 km (68 and 150 miles) up emits various shades of green. Oxygen at higher altitudes glows a beautiful ruby-red.

124

Aurora
Ground view

The most common form of aurora is a long, thin curtain.
When viewed from a distance, this luminous curtain makes
an arc across the poleward horizon. Also known as the
northern and southern lights, auroras are concentrated
in a roughly circular zone, known as the *auroral oval*,
located about one-fourth of the way from the north or
south geomagnetic pole to the equator. In the Northern
Hemisphere, the auroral zone passes over central Alaska,
northern Canada, the northern tip of Scandinavia, and
part of Siberia. The majority of people on Earth live too
far from the auroral oval to witness auroras regularly.
Auroral activity increases every 11 years, at the peak of
the sunspot cycle, and at these times auroras sometimes
extend far away from the poles and appear in mid-latitude
skies. The most recent such peak in auroral activity
occurred in 1989. Often at mid-latitudes the aurora is
partly below the horizon, and only the upper part of the
auroral curtain is visible, giving the appearance of a false
dawn—thus it was named for Aurora, the Roman goddess
of the dawn.

126

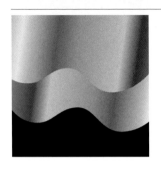

Aurora
Ground view

Auroral lights in the north are known as *aurora borealis,* those in the south as *aurora australis.* The folded curtain structure of the northern lights is beautifully illustrated in this spectacular photograph, which also contains the seven stars of the Big Dipper. These shimmering curtains of light present a constantly changing display, as the luminous streaks trace Earth's magnetic field lines. Earth's magnetic field is shaped like a dipole, as if the center of Earth contained a large bar magnet. If the magnetic field were not affected by the flow of charged particles from the Sun, known as the solar wind, the magnetic field lines would symmetrically plunge toward Earth's surface near the north and south geomagnetic poles, and curve so as to be parallel to the surface near the equator. However, the solar wind compresses the magnetic field lines on the sunward side of Earth, and draws them out into an elongated tail on the opposite side In this elongated tail, those magnetic field lines poleward of the auroral oval become disconnected, allowing charged particles access to the upper atmosphere.

128

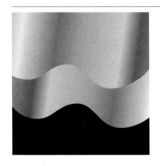

Aurora
Space shuttle Discovery *photograph*

The astronauts aboard space shuttle *Discovery* Mission 39 obtained this impressive image of the aurora australis, or southern lights, in the spring of 1991. One of the objectives of this mission was to study whether or not auroras could be confused with missile plumes by early-warning satellites. The shuttle had a low orbital altitude of 260 km (160 miles), within the altitude range in which auroras naturally occur, and was placed in a high inclination orbit that took it close to the polar regions. The aurora grades upward along the magnetic field lines to an indistinct top margin, but shows a sharp lower boundary near the base of the ionosphere—a layer where many of the atoms that make up Earth's atmosphere have lost electrons due to interactions with ultraviolet radiation, solar wind, and cosmic rays. The reddish color near the top of the aurora is due to emission by oxygen atoms. A faint reddish band, called *airglow,* can be seen just below the ionosphere; it is caused by light given off when atoms combine to form molecules.

THE MOON

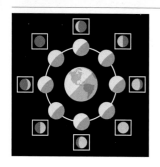

Full Moon
Ground view

The full moon has always fired the human imagination. This lunar phase was reputed to induce madness in some people (who came to be known as lunatics), to turn others into wolfmen, and to influence events such as births and accidents. The full moon is bright and up all night, rising at sunset and setting at dawn. Most of the features on the nearside of the Moon can be observed at the full phase, but as the sunlight hits it directly, no shadows or surface depth are visible. The best times to observe the lunar surface are before and after full moon, when shadows cast by lunar mountains and cliffs can be seen with binoculars and small telescopes along the terminator, the dividing line between the illuminated part and the dark part. Observers of the Moon can readily distinguish two types of terrain: the dark, irregular patches called *maria,* or seas (singular *mare*), lava plains that long ago solidified into dark basaltic rock, and the lighter, mountainous areas called *lunar highlands.* The lunar maps that accompany the first- and third-quarter moon photographs on pages 148–151 will help you identify lunar features.

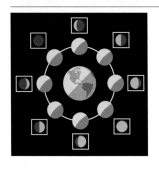

Moon: Waxing Gibbous
Ground view

Our Moon is made visible to us by the Sun's light shining on it. The side or hemisphere of the Moon that faces the Sun is lit, while the opposite side is dark. The Moon's appearance changes from night to night, exhibiting what we call lunar phases, because as the Moon orbits Earth it presents to us changing perspectives on its day side. At *new moon,* when the Moon is directly between Earth and the Sun, the unlit hemisphere faces Earth, so the Moon is not visible. During the week following new moon, the edge of the Moon's illuminated side comes into view, creating a *waxing crescent* moon, followed by a *first-quarter* moon, with half the day side and half the night side presented to Earth. In the week after the first-quarter phase, more than half the lit side can be seen, giving us a *waxing gibbous* phase, as in this photograph. When Earth is directly between the Sun and the Moon, we see the entire lit half of the Moon, visible as a *full moon.* Over the two weeks after full moon the phases reverse, back through *waning gibbous, third quarter* (last quarter), and *waning crescent* to new moon.

136

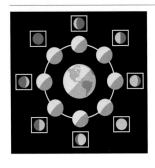

New Moon: Solar Eclipse
Ground view

In the new moon phase, the Moon is positioned between Earth and the Sun, and its unlit side faces Earth. The Moon and the Sun are more or less aligned from our viewpoint and they rise and set at the same time. Thus, the new moon is in the sky all day, right next to the Sun, so we can't see it. During a solar eclipse the location of the new moon becomes clear, as seen in this photograph, taken at sunset on January 4, 1992, of the shadow of the new moon blocking the Sun's disk. A solar eclipse can occur only when the new moon crosses the *ecliptic*, the plane defined by Earth's orbit around the Sun (called the ecliptic because eclipses, lunar or solar, happen only when the Moon is aligned with the Sun and Earth in this plane). The Moon's orbital plane is tilted $5\frac{1}{2}°$ to the ecliptic, so the Moon crosses Earth's orbital plane twice each month, but not always at the time of new or full phase. This photograph shows an annular eclipse, in which a ring of the Sun's disk remains in view. This occurs when the Moon is at the point in its orbit at which it is farthest from Earth.

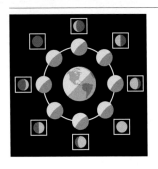

Moon: Waxing Crescent
Ground view

On some nights just before or after new moon, when the Moon is a very thin crescent, the darkened part of the disk is faintly illuminated. This phenomenon, sometimes called "ashen light of the Moon" or, more romantically, "the old Moon in the new Moon's arms," is caused by *earthshine*, sunlight reflected off Earth's atmosphere. Earthshine is brightest when Earth's day side has a cloud covering, which serves as a reflector. If you were standing on the Moon as it is photographed here, the Earth would appear at near full phase and would be quite bright. The line separating the sunlit part of the Moon from the dark part which gradually sweeps across the Moon's face as the lunar phases progress, is known as the *terminator*. If the surface of the Moon were completely featureless, the terminator would trace out a smooth curve, but lunar mountains and valleys catch the light and throw shadows. In this photograph an irregularity in the terminator, about one-third the way down, marks the location of the mountains surrounding Mare Crisium, one of the Moon's "seas" (ancient lava plains).

140

Lunar Eclipse
Time-sequence photograph

A lunar eclipse, during which the Moon passes into Earth's shadow, occurs when the Moon is full and the Sun, Earth, and Moon are in a direct line. The orbit of the Moon is tilted relative to the plane of Earth's orbit around the Sun (the ecliptic), so most full moons are slightly out of alignment with the Sun and Earth, and no eclipse occurs. This time-sequence photograph shows the unfolding of a total lunar eclipse. (The trails of spots above and below the Moon's image are multiple exposures of bright stars.) First the Moon moves into Earth's *penumbra* (outer shadow) and darkens almost imperceptibly. *First contact* occurs when the eastern limb of the Moon just touches Earth's *umbra* (inner shadow). Then the Moon moves deeper and deeper into the shadow until it reaches *second contact,* the beginning of *totality* (when it is completely covered by the shadow). Totality, during which the Moon usually takes on a deep reddish color, can last as long as 1¾ hours. The end of totality, when the Moon begins to emerge from the shadow, is called *third contact.* At *fourth contact* the eclipse is over.

142

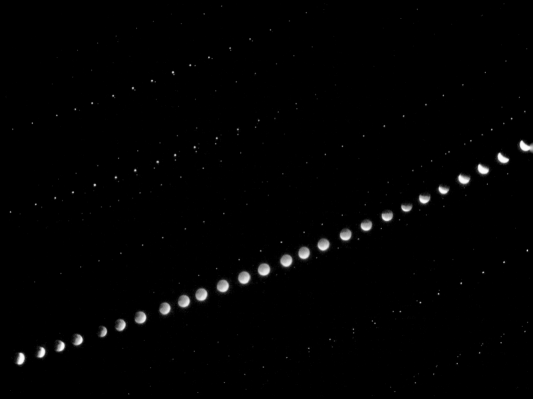

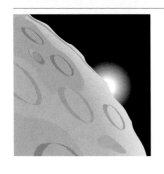

Occultation of Jupiter
Time-sequence photographs

An occultation occurs when a moon or planet passes in front of and totally eclipses another object (for example, a star, a different moon, or a planet). In this pair of photographs, our Moon is occulting Jupiter, the largest planet in the solar system. (Jupiter's diameter is more than 11 times greater than Earth's; the giant planet is approximately 2,000 times farther away from Earth than the Moon is, which is why it looks so small in this image.) The dark and pale bands of Jupiter's upper atmosphere can be discerned in this photograph, but the slightly greenish hue is inaccurate. An occultation is a powerful tool in astronomy, enabling researchers to determine the sizes of many objects. Rings were discovered around Uranus and Neptune by ground-based observations of occultations of stars by these two planets before the rings were confirmed by *Voyager* spacecraft images. A *grazing occultation* occurs when the Moon just skims an object, such as a star. Observers may see the star move across the limb of the Moon, disappearing behind lunar mountains and reappearing through valleys.

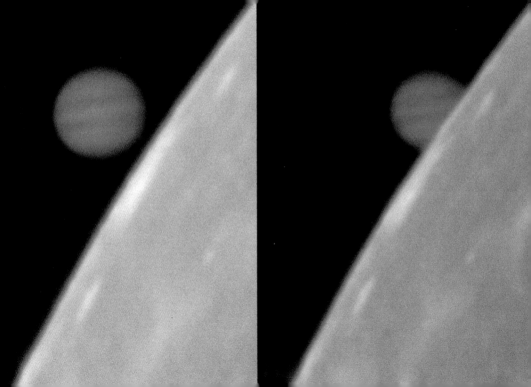

Lunar Geography: First-Quarter Moon

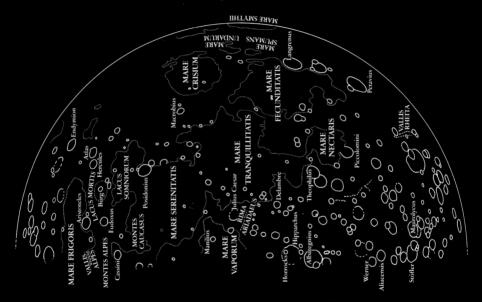

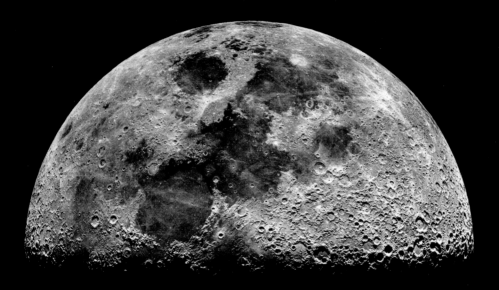

Lunar Geography: Third-Quarter Moon

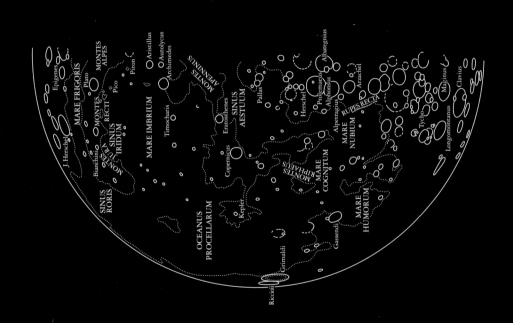

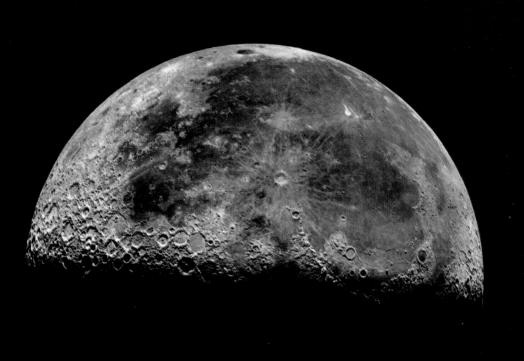

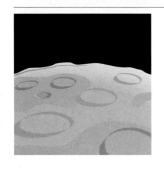

Mare Imbrium
Earth-based telescope photograph

The Moon's two general surface types—*maria* (singular *mare*) and *highlands*—are so distinctive they can be seen from Earth with the naked eye. The lighter areas are highlands, mountainous, cratered terrain almost 4.5 billion years old. The relatively smooth maria, the dark blotches on the Moon's face, are within huge basins hundreds of miles across that were excavated about 3.9 billion years ago by the impacts of debris left over from the solar system's formation. Subsequent lava flows erupted from the Moon's upper mantle and filled in the basins over a long period that ended 3.1 billion years ago. The lava solidified, turning into basaltic rock, which gives the maria their characteristic darkness. Mare Imbrium was the last of these large basins to be filled in. The basin's rim includes the Montes Alpes (the Alps), in the upper right, and the Montes Apenninus (the Apennines), located along the lower right. In the interior of Mare Imbrium, adjacent to the Apennines, is the light-colored, rough-textured Apennine Bench, made of volcanic deposits that were too high to be covered by the basalt flows that filled the rest of the basin.

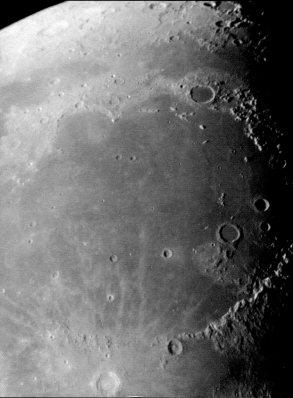

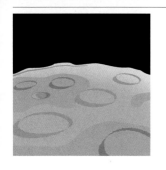

Copernicus Crater
Lunar Orbiter IV *photograph*

Copernicus, in the upper left of this image, is an 800-million-year-old lunar *impact crater* for which the Copernican Period, the most recent of the Moon's geologic periods, was named. Impacts by small objects produced simple, bowl-shaped craters, such as the one in the upper right. Huge impacts produced multi-ringed basins like the Orientale Basin. Impacting objects of intermediate size produced such craters as Copernicus (93 km/58 miles wide), with a terraced rim and one or more central peaks. A *terrace* is produced when the inside of a crater rim slumps under its own weight. Central peaks are formed by interactions of shock waves as the crater is excavated (blasted out by the impact); the peaks in Copernicus consist of material brought up from great depths. *Ejecta* (particles of material ejected on impact) form the rough, rolling apron of debris immediately surrounding the crater. Farther from the crater, the ejecta cool and separate into discrete clumps that produce strings of secondary craters when they hit the ground, as seen in the right margin of this image.

154

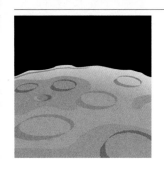

Tycho Crater
Lunar Orbiter IV *photograph*

A prominent lunar crater located in the southern highlands, Tycho (85 km/53 miles in diameter), in the bottom center of this image, is close to Copernicus in size and has a terraced rim and central peaks. Several chains of secondary craters, created by ejecta (ejected matter) from Tycho, are aligned radially to the crater; some of them are quite prominent. When seen from a distance, Tycho's ejecta form the largest crater "rays" on the Moon. None of the *Apollo* missions landed near Tycho, but *Surveyor 7* landed about 40 km (25 miles) away from it. *Surveyor* sent back images of a rolling, hilly terrain covered by numerous angular rocks and boulders. The age of this relatively young crater (about 100 million years) was determined from *Apollo 17* samples of debris from a landslide off South Massif, a mountain adjacent to the Taurus Littrow valley, along the edge of Mare Serenitatis. This landslide was triggered by the impact of ejecta from Tycho, 2,250 km (1,400 miles) to the southwest. Material excavated by impacts travels great distances on the Moon because of the low gravity and the absence of atmospheric drag.

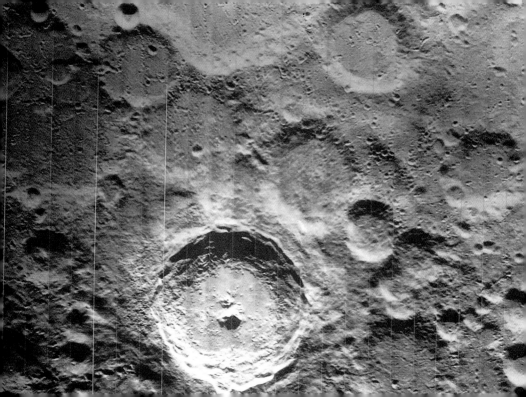

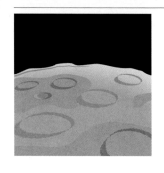

Montes Apenninus
Apollo 15 *orbital photograph*

The Montes Apenninus (the Appenines), among the highest mountains on the Moon (up to 4,600 meters/ 15,000 feet) are believed to be part of the outermost ring of the giant, multi-ringed Imbrium basin. The Apenninus range consists of uplifted pre-Imbrium bedrock and ejecta thrown out by the impact that formed the basin late in the period of intense bombardment in the solar system, about 3.5 billion years ago. Ejecta are material ejected when a meteoroid or asteroid hits a surface. Rocky in nature, the ejecta may be heated to melting or even vaporization by the energy of the impact. The *Apollo 15* mission landed near the Apenninus mountains and collected rock samples, mostly breccias, made up of fragments from different sources that have been mixed together and cemented by impact processes. Some of the breccias are a mixture of extremely old rock fragments (up to 4.48 billion years old) and solidified impact melt material (3.85 billion years old). Also recovered was a chunk of anorthrosite called the Genesis rock, probably a fragment of the Moon's original crust.

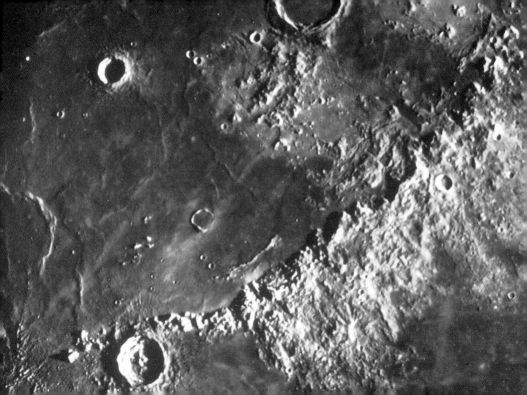

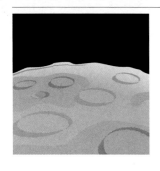

Vallis Alpes
Lunar Orbiter V *photograph*

This oblique view looks southwestward across the Montes Alpes, which formed at the same time and in the same manner as the Montes Apenninus and consist of a combination of uplifted crustal blocks and ejecta from the Imbrium impact. The large, flat-bottomed valley in the middle of the image, the Alpes valley cuts across the Alpes mountains for a distance of 190 km (118 miles). The valley is oriented radially to the Imbrium basin, and is bordered on both sides by parallel faults. The area between the two faults has dropped downward as a result of movement along the faults, forming a depressed segment of crust known as a *graben*. The radial orientation of the graben is due to the force of the impact that created the Imbrium basin. After the valley formed, its bottom surface was flooded by lava. The sinuous *rille* down the center of the Alpes valley resembles similar channels found elsewhere on the Moon and on the island of Hawaii, where they served as pathways for flowing lava, which either cleared out or crusted over during the flow, then subsequently collapsed.

160

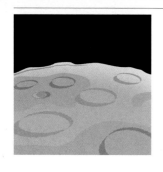

Volcano and Impact Craters
Apollo 16 *orbital photograph*

Since the advent of space exploration, we have learned that virtually all craters on the Moon were created by impacts, although a few volcanic craters have been found. Impact craters have a sharply defined raised rim and a surrounding blanket of debris, known as ejecta, which has a concave profile. Two large impact craters are visible in the lower left of this oblique view of an area in Mare Nubium. The larger of the two craters is about 3 km (1.9 miles) across. The smaller is surrounded by a bright ejecta blanket, indicative of its relative youth. Just left of the photograph's center is an extinct volcano. It can be distinguished from the impact craters by its rim, which is convex in shape and projects higher above the surrounding plains than the rims of the impact craters. The volcanic crater was formed by the eruption of pyroclastic (ash-like) materials. A scalloped-shaped *wrinkle ridge* is visible to the right of the volcano. Often associated with lunar volcanism, wrinkle ridges are believed to have formed when surface material contracted as it solidified, causing thrust faults (broken sections forced over other sections).

162

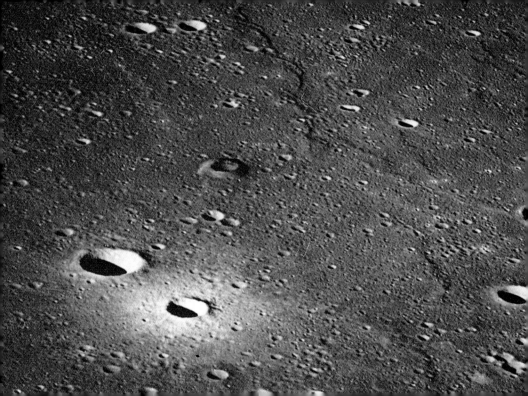

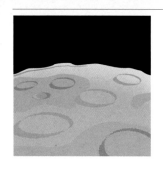

Camelot Crater
Apollo 17 lunar surface photograph

This photograph of a rock-strewn landscape was taken during *Apollo 17*, the last manned mission to the Moon. The depression behind the large boulders to the left is Camelot crater, which is 650 meters (2,000 feet) across. Because the Moon has no atmosphere and hence no weather, the astronauts' bootprints, visible in the lower right, will remain for millions of years. The rocks surrounding Camelot crater, ranging in size from small cobbles to boulders 1 meter (3 feet) across, are basalts from a lava flow. During solidification, dissolved gases escaped from the cooling lava, forming pockets, known as vesicles, in the rock that are visible as holes in the surface. Originally buried as deep as 130 meters (420 feet) by later lava flows, these basalts were excavated by the impact that created Camelot crater some 100 million years ago. Such impacts, by bringing up rocks from deep within the Moon's crust, supplied astronauts with sample materials from a variety of depths otherwise inaccessible. The basalts collected at Camelot crater are 3.8 billion years old, among the oldest basalts recovered during the Apollo program.

164

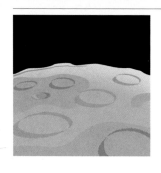

Hadley Rille from Space
Apollo 15 *orbital photograph*

This image of Hadley Rille was taken from orbit, just before the *Apollo 15* landing module descended toward the lunar surface. From the left (south) side of the image, the rille trends northeast and abruptly turns toward the northwest at bottom center. The landing site is below the first kink (named "the Terrace") to the right of this abrupt change of direction, about 2 km (1.2 miles) away from the rille. The large, dark circular region to the lower left (southeast) of the rille is an impact crater, St. George (about 1.5 km/.9 miles in diameter). A major objective of the *Apollo 15* mission was to determine the origin of Hadley Rille, a sinuous valley that extends some 100 km (60 miles) from a volcanic crater on the flank of the Apenninus mountains into the Imbrium basin. Based on the results of this mission, Hadley Rille is believed to be either an open channel that once contained flowing lava or a collapsed lava tube—a subsurface channel whose roof later gave way. Both types of lava channels are also associated with basaltic volcanism on Earth.

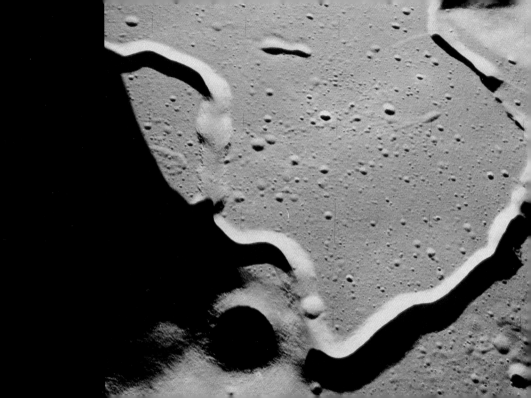

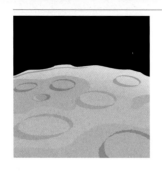

Astronaut at Hadley Rille
Apollo 15 *lunar surface photograph*

This image, featuring astronaut Dave Scott and the *Apollo 15* lunar rover at the edge of Hadley Rille, was taken from the flank of St. George crater, looking northwestward along the valley, which at this location is 1.4 km (.8 mile) wide and 350 meters (1,150 feet) deep. The fine powder that covers the lunar surface, reaching depths of 20 meters (65 feet), is evident in the foreground. The astronauts also took an excursion to the Terrace (the first illuminated wall of the rille visible on the right-hand side of this image), the only place on the Moon where they extracted samples of intact bedrock. All other rock samples obtained during the six Apollo landings had been moved by impacts. These bedrock rock samples, basalts, proved to be 3.3 billion years old. Across the rille from the Terrace, astronauts saw 60 meters (200 feet) of layered basalt lava flows along the valley's uppermost walls. The topmost flow was a thick, massive layer containing columns that form when cooling basalts shrink and fracture vertically. Beneath this uppermost flow were 8 to 12 thin layers of darker-colored basalt flows.

168

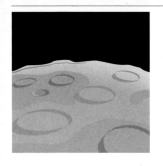

Grabens and Volcanic Deposits
Apollo 16 *orbital photograph*

This image shows a mix of lunar topography. The ridge of mountains arcing across the center separates two large impact craters, Bonpland (entire right side) and Fra Mauro (upper left area), that were later flooded with lava. A linear valley—a graben—cuts across the rim into each. Along the margin of the Bonpland graben is a line of small dark hills about 8 km (5 miles) long surrounded by material that buried the graben and the surrounding impact craters. Superposition relationships (younger features atop older ones) reveal the geologic history of the area. Sometime after lava flooded the impact craters, the graben, a feature created when crust drops between two parallel faults, formed perpendicular to the ridge. At a later time the graben in Bonpland was covered with pyroclastic deposits. These deposits of ashlike material, darker in appearance than the mare basalts, were ejected from the dark hills, which are extinct, partially buried volcanoes that are probably cinder cones. The small, irregularly shaped crater at upper left is also believed to be a volcanic crater.

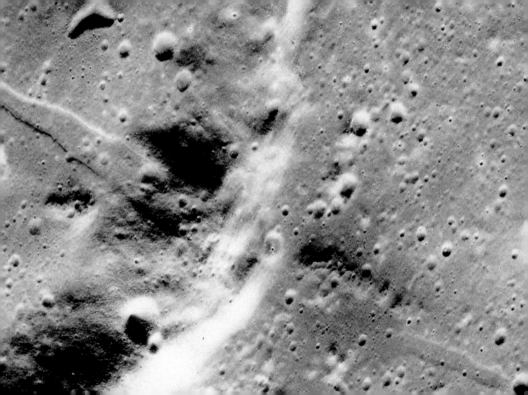

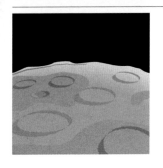

Split Rock
Apollo 17 lunar surface photograph

Orbital photographs were used to scope out the landing site of *Apollo 17* at Taurus Littrow, a valley along the edge of Mare Serenitatis. A boulder at the end of a trackway that started one-third of the way up a mountain, North Massif, near the edge of Mare Serenitatis, was visible in the photographs. It had apparently broken loose from North Massif and rolled toward the plain below. It was decided that the astronauts would land near this boulder, which came to be called Split Rock (shown here with astronaut Harrison Schmitt), and take samples from it. The rock's two halves, discovered to be solidified impact melts (probably from the same impact that excavated the Serenitatis basin), had different appearances. The half nearest Schmitt is bluish and crystalline; the other half is greener and more vesicular (marked by air pockets). The blue half contains white clasts (broken-up fragments) of highland rock that preexisted impact melting. The green half has white clasts as well as fragments of the blue rock, evidence that it must have been the last of the sampled material to solidify.

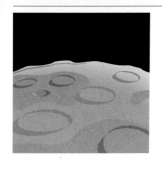

Orientale Basin
Lunar Orbiter IV *photograph*

The Orientale basin, here seen from the Moon's farside, is just beyond the eastern limb of the 59 percent of the lunar surface visible from Earth. Orientale is the youngest large, multi-ringed basin on the Moon. All large impact basins on the Moon are believed to have resembled Orientale before subsequent flooding by lava, including those underlying the maria on the nearside. The dark circular area on the right is Grimaldi crater, completely filled in with dark basaltic lava. Oceanus Procellarum is the dark area to the upper right. The outermost ring of the basin, the Cordillera Mountains, is 930 km (578 miles) across. The next ring in, the Rook Mountains, is 620 km (385 miles) across. Outside the Cordillera Mountains, particularly near the terminator, radial structures—elongated ridges and valleys—are apparent. Such structures, formed by ejecta from the basin, are found up to 600 km (373 miles) from the Cordillera Mountains. Small, dark Mare Orientale is visible in the center of the basin (bottom edge), and smaller mare patches are visible on the inner edges of the mountains.

174

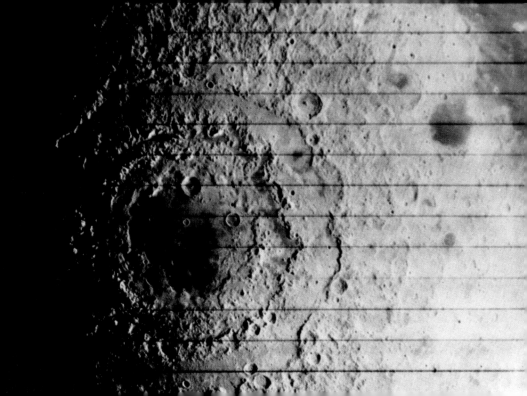

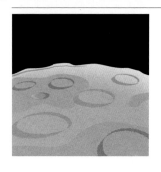

The Moon's Eastern Limb
Galileo *orbital photograph*

This unfamiliar view of the Moon, showing both farside and nearside, was photographed in December 1990 by *Galileo* during one of its two flybys of Earth and the Moon before the "gravitational slingshot" boosts by Venus, Earth, and the Moon gave it the velocity to reach its intended target, Jupiter. Some of the farside seen here is actually occasionally visible from Earth, thanks to lunar libration, which slightly changes our perspective of the Moon as it orbits Earth and enables us to see 59 percent of the lunar surface over time. In the center of the image is the huge Orientale impact basin, the only large basin on the Moon that was not wholly flooded by lava. Small amounts of the dark basalt that results from lava flows are visible in Mare Orientale, in the center of the basin. Numerous small young craters with bright ejecta blankets are visible in the area surrounding Orientale. The dark region to the upper right of the image is Oceanus Procellarum, located on the side of the Moon that faces Earth. Barely visible in the lower left is a remnant of the largest lunar impact basin yet discovered, first seen in images sent by *Galileo*.

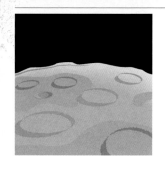

The Moon's Farside: Korolev Crater
Apollo 8 *orbital photograph*

This bleak view of the ancient highlands terrain on the lunar farside was taken by the astronauts of *Apollo 8* as they made one of their 10 orbits around the Moon in December 1968, seven months before the first lunar landing. The image covers an area 32 km (20 miles) wide on the floor of Korolev crater, a large depression named after Soviet rocket designer Sergei Korolev. The roughness of the crater floor, accentuated by the low angle of the sunlight on the surface, is typical of the farside, most of which is completely saturated with craters. There are no large maria on the farside, and the elevation is much higher than on the side that faces Earth. Astronomers speculate that the farside has a thicker crust that withstood the impacts of large meteoroids that might have broken through thinner areas of crust and caused the mare-forming lava to well up. The farside's older craters show subdued rims, while younger craters have crisply defined rims. Many of the small, sharply defined craters in this image are believed to be secondary craters created by the ejecta from the impact that formed the nearby Orientale basin.

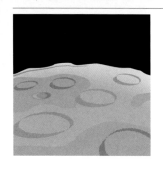

The Moon's Farside: Tsiolkovsky Crater
Apollo 13 *orbital photograph*

This oblique view of the farside crater Tsiolkovsky was taken by the crew of *Apollo 13* as they flew by the Moon. Most of the features on the lunar farside are named after famous Soviets, as this region was first photographed by the Soviet Union. This one is named for a late 19th-century Russian rocket pioneer. (Nearside features are named for scientists and thinkers of the Western world.) Tsiolkovsky crater is one of the most noticeable features on the Moon's farside because of the contrast between the dark basalt, rarely found on the lunar farside, that partly fills the crater's floor and the light-colored highlands that comprise most of the farside landscape. Debris slumping off the crater's terraced wall fell into and partly filled the crater before the flooding by lava. The central peak, common in large lunar impact craters, consists of material brought up from a great depth by the interactions of shock waves generated by the impact. The surrounding terrain visible in this image shows the farside's typical pockmarked surface, with newer craters partially obliterating existing ones.

182

Solar Imaging

The Sun is our link to the stars of the cosmos. It is the only star whose surface and atmosphere we can see clearly and directly. Its basic properties, such as mass, size, age, temperature, luminosity, chemical composition, atmospheric turbulence, rotation, and magnetic field strength, offer clues to the properties of other stars. Such phenomena as sunspots, flares, spicules, prominences, coronal streamers and holes, granulation, and large-scale motions in the photosphere can all be seen directly from Earth. Astronomers use many different techniques to study and observe the Sun. A few of them are briefly described below.

White-light Photography

White-light, or visible-light, images of the Sun, taken in natural light but with special filters to tone down its blinding brightness, are useful for recording activity in the photosphere, such as sunspots.

Narrow-band Color Filters

Narrow-band color filters allow only a small range of wavelengths to pass to the recorder and are useful for capturing photospheric, chromospheric, and coronal activities. These filters are specific to the wavelength of a particular absorption, or emission, line of a given chemical element's spectrum. They let through only the specific colors emitted by that element, highlighting different aspects of the Sun's makeup. The K line of calcium, for example, can be used to reveal the strength of solar flare activity. The hydrogen alpha line (Hα) can display chromospheric spicules and flare and prominence activity in the lower corona. One helium infrared line can be used to map activities in the Sun's outer corona, such as coronal holes.

Other Energy Wavelengths

Among the other energy wavelengths at which astronomers view the sky are X ray, gamma ray, ultraviolet, and radio, some of which cannot penetrate Earth's atmosphere and must be recorded with space-based equipment.

Coronagraphs

A coronagraph, a telescope equipped with a disk that completely blocks out the Sun's disk, creating in effect an artificial solar eclipse, is used for studying the corona as well as prominences. With the intense light from the photosphere obscured, the light from the fainter corona comes through, enabling scientists to study its changing shape and intensity. A coronagraph is often used in conjunction with a narrow-band color filter, allowing a specific aspect of the corona to be observed.

Magnetograms

Magnetograms, which record magnetic fields, are made by combining two images generated at wavelengths on either side of a magnetically split spectral line. These images can reveal in detail the strengths and directions of magnetic fields and related sunspot activity (even activity that is not yet detectable in visible light) and solar flares.

Spectrograms

Spectrographs, which disperse radiation into a spectrum and then record the results, can supply images of the Sun's spectrum—called spectrograms—with the highest wavelength resolutions possible. Astronomers interpret the spectrum to determine chemical composition, atmospheric temperatures, large-scale motions, pressure and turbulence, and magnetic fields on the Sun.

False-color Imaging

False colors are added to images obtained in many of the above-mentioned ways in order to highlight their different aspects. False colors are used to bring out differences in brightness, to reveal temperature gradients, or to indicate magnetic polarity, among other uses.

Sun: Basic Data

Distance:	149,597,870 km (92,955,800 miles; 107 solar diameters) from Earth	*Rotation:*	25 days (equatorial regions) to 35 days (polar regions)
Diameter:	1,392,530 km (865,280 miles); 109 Earth diameters	*Magnitude:*	−26.7
Mass:	332,946 × Earth's mass	*Luminosity:*	3.85×10^{26} watts
Density:	1.41 gm/cm³ (density of H_2O = 1 gm/cm³)	*Spectral type:*	G2 V
"Surface" gravity:	27.9 × Earth's gravity; escape velocity (speed an object has to travel to escape gravitational pull): 617.5 km/sec (Earth's = 11.2 km/sec)	*Temperature:*	Surface (photosphere): 5800°K; core: 15,000,000°K
		Composition:	By particle count: 92.1% hydrogen, 7.8% helium, 0.1% heavier elements; all in a gaseous state, virtually all ionized (plasma)

Moon: Basic Data

Distance:	Average: 384,400 km (239,000 miles) from Earth; perigee (nearest): 356,400 km (221,460 miles); apogee (farthest): 406,700 km (252,710 miles)
Diameter:	3,476 km (2,160 miles); 0.273 Earth diameters
Mass:	0.01230 × Earth's mass
Density:	3.34 gm/cm³ (density of H_2O = 1 gm/cm³; density of Earth = 5.52 gm/cm³)
Surface gravity:	0.17 × Earth's gravity; escape velocity (speed an object has to travel to escape gravitational pull): 2.4 km/sec (Earth's = 11.2 km/sec)
Rotation:	27.322 days

Eccentricity of orbit:	0.055, based on a scale of 0 (perfect circle) to 1 (maximum elongated ellipse)
Orbital velocity:	3,680 km/hr (2,280 mph)
Inclination of orbit:	5.5° to plane of Earth's orbit (ecliptic)
Axial tilt:	6.7° to plane of Moon's orbit
Sidereal period:	27.32166 days (one full revolution around Earth)
Synodic period:	29.53059 days (full cycle of lunar phases)
Magnitude:	−12.7 at full moon
Temperature:	Surface: −150°C to 100°C (−200°F to 212°F)

Solar Eclipses

This table lists all the annular (A) and total (T) solar eclipses from 1995 to 2010. The approximate time at mid-eclipse is given here in eastern standard time (EST) on the 24-hour clock. The duration indicates the maximum length (minutes:seconds) of the total or annular phase (it varies according to the viewer's location).

Date	EST at mid-eclipse	Type	Duration	Region of Visibility
1995 Apr 29	13:00	A	6:38	Pacific, Central and South America
1995 Oct 24	00:00	T	2:10	S Asia, Japan, Pacific
1997 Mar 8	20:00	T	2:50	E Asia, Siberia
1998 Feb 26	12:00	T	4:08	Pacific, N South America, Atlantic
1998 Aug 21	21:00	A	3:14	S Asia, Indonesia, Pacific
1999 Feb 16	02:00	A	1:19	Indian Ocean, Australia
1999 Aug 11	06:00	T	2:23	Atlantic, Europe, SE and S Asia
2001 Jun 21	07:00	T	4:56	S Atlantic, S Africa, Madagascar
2001 Dec 14	16:00	A	3:54	Pacific, Central America
2002 Jun 10	19:00	A	1:13	Pacific
2002 Dec 4	03:00	T	2:04	S Africa, Indian Ocean, Australia
2003 May 30	23:00	A	3:37	Iceland, Arctic
2003 Nov 23	18:00	T	1:57	South Pacific, Antarctica
2005 Apr 8	16:00	A,T	0:42	Pacific, N South America
2005 Oct 3	06:00	A	4:32	Atlantic, Spain, Africa
2006 Mar 29	05:00	T	4:07	Atlantic, Africa, Turkey, Asia
2006 Sep 22	07:00	A	7:09	NE South America, Atlantic
2008 Feb 6	23:00	A	2:14	S Pacific, Antarctica
2008 Aug 1	05:00	T	2:28	N Canada, Arctic, Siberia
2009 Jan 29	03:00	A	7:56	S Atlantic, Indian Ocean
2010 Jul 11	15:00	T	5:18	Pacific

Lunar Eclipses

This table lists partial (P) and total (T) lunar eclipses from 1995 to 2010. The time of the eclipse at the height of totality is given here in eastern standard time (EST) on the 24-hour clock. Duration of totality and length of total eclipse are given in hours and minutes (hours : minutes).

Date	EST at mid-eclipse	Type	Duration of totality	Length of Eclipse
1995 Apr 15	07:19	P	—	1:12
1996 Apr 3	19:11	T	1:26	3:36
1996 Sep 26	21:55	T	1:10	3:22
1997 Mar 23	23:41	P	—	3:22
1997 Sep 16	13:47	T	1:02	3:16
1999 Jul 28	06:34	P	—	2:22
2000 Jan 20	23:45	T	1:16	3:22
2000 Jul 16	08:57	T	1:46	3:56
2001 Jan 9	15:22	T	1:00	3:16
2001 Jul 5	09:57	P	—	2:38
2003 May 15	22:41	T	0:52	3:14
2003 Nov 8	20:20	T	0:22	3:30
2004 May 4	15:32	T	1:16	3:22
2004 Oct 27	22:05	T	1:20	3:38
2005 Oct 17	07:04	P	—	0:56
2006 Sep 7	13:52	P	—	1:30
2007 Mar 3	18:22	T	1:14	3:40
2007 Aug 28	05:38	T	1:30	3:32
2008 Feb 20	22:27	T	0:50	3:24
2008 Aug 16	16:11	P	—	3:08
2009 Dec 31	14:24	P	—	1:00
2010 Jun 26	06:40	P	—	2:42
2010 Dec 21	03:18	T	1:12	3:28

Index

Credits

Photographers

ALASKA STOCK IMAGES:
John Warden (129)

ASTROSTOCK*SANFORD:
Daniel Fisher (139)
John Sanford (141, 153)

Lee C. Coombs (27, 135, 147)
Akira Fujii (101)
Richard Hill (119, 137)
Shirley M. Holle (115)
Jet Propulsion Lab (177)
Richard Keen (145)
Bob King (103)
Lick Observatory (149, 151)
Lunar and Planetary Lab (157, 161, 163, 165, 167, 169, 171)
Courtesy NASA (25, 81, 93, 95, 131, 155, 159, 175, 179, 181, 183)
Courtesy NASA from the slide set Planetary Systems by the Astronomical Society of the Pacific (173)
National Optical Astronomy Observatories (53, 55, 57, 59, 61, 63, 65, 67, 69, 71, 73, 75, 77, 79, 83, 85, 87, 89, 97)
National Solar Observatory (91)
Pekka Parviainen (123, 125, 127, 143)

PETER ARNOLD, INC.:
Fred Bruemmer (29)
Richard J. Wainscoat (99)

PHOTO RESEARCHERS:
© Michael Giannechini (117)

Steve Warble (121)
Patrick Wiggins/Hansen Planetarium (105, 107, 109, 111, 113)

Cover Photograph: Annular eclipse, by Daniel Fisher/Astrostock*Sanford
Title Page: Sunrise, by Lee C. Coombs
Pages 22–23: Sun pillar, by Steve Warble
Pages 132–133: Moonrise over Chugach Mountains, by Bruce M. Herman/Photo Researchers

Staff

This book was created by Chanticleer Press. All editorial inquiries should be addressed to:
Chanticleer Press
568 Broadway, #1005A
New York, NY 10012
(212) 941-1522

To purchase this book, or other National Audubon Society illustrated nature books, please contact:
Alfred A. Knopf, Inc.
201 East 50th Street
New York, NY 10022
(800) 733-3000

Chanticleer Press Staff

Publisher: Andrew Stewart
Managing Editor: Edie Locke
Art Director: Amanda Wilson
Production Manager: Susan Schoenfeld
Photo Editor: Giema Tsakuginow
Photo Assistant: C. Tiffany Lee
Publishing Assistant: Alicia Mills
Text Editors: Amy K. Hughes and Patricia Fogarty
Natural Science Consultant: Richard Keen
Picture Editor: Alexandra Truitt
Picture Researcher: Jerry Marshall
Illustrations: Acme Design
Original series design by Massimo Vignelli

Founding Publisher: Paul Steiner